Gerard Kelly is an author, poet, thinker, evangelist and pastor who currently runs a centre for missional spirituality in France. He regularly speaks at large Christian gatherings and is author of a number of books including *Breakfast with God* and *Twitturgies*. He is a leader of the Bless Network, www.blessnet.eu

"Gerard's fusion of theology, philosophy and poetry offers a great read!"
    – **Dave Wiles, CEO of Frontier Youth Trust and author, *Stories from The Edge***

"I can't think of a more timely, important or indeed prophetic exploration of God at work amongst his people."
    – **Steve Clifford, General Director, Evangelical Alliance**

"An important book. Buy it. Read it. Reflect on it. And let the living colours of its message warm you at the fire of God's greatest idea ever."
    – **Danielle Strickland, Salvation Army, Canada, and author, *The Liberating Truth*: *How Jesus Empowers Women***

"A joy to read. Many authors on the subject of the church become fixated with models of church. Gerard explores the essence of the church. Inspiring."
    – **Martin Robinson, National Director, Together in Mission, and Principal of Springdale College**

"*Church Actually* blazes with artistry and life. It is England's Guy Fawkes Night and America's Independence Day all rolled into one fizzing, popping read. A dazzling book."
    – **Viv Thomas, Director of Formation, St. Paul's Hammersmith, and author of *The Spectacular Ordinary Life***

"A marvellous picture of the church as God always has planned for it to be. A must read."
    – **Paul Francis, Leader, Glenwood Church, Cardiff**

"Gerard is a poet of the Spirit. He holds before us the romance and the reality of what church is meant to be. It is a book I have longed to see. I love it."
    – **David White, Vicar, St Andrew's Chorleywood**

"Sparkles with humour, cut-diamond insights and inspiration. In this delightful book Gerard offers original suggestions as to how church can become (once again) colourful, winsome and fruitful."
    – **Mark Roques, Director of RealityBites, and author, *Fields of God***

"Sprinkled with creative illustrations and provocative metaphors, this work of art deserves to be studied by everyone trying to create something beautiful for God."
    – **David Lawrence, Inspire Network, and author of *Heaven: It's Not the End of the World***

"Sheer genius. Gerard celebrates all that is good about the church. He is such a gifted writer."
    – **Debra Green, National Director, Redeemin**

"Do we really believe that the church is God's mast pictures of God's brilliant vision."
    – **Martin Lee, Director, Global Connections**

D0492289

"Reminds us that the church is God's brilliant idea: a place of new community, of passion and love, where people share their humanity together and celebrate the presence of God… invigorating."
    – **Pete Phillips, Director of Research, CODEC, St John's College Durham**

"Creative and inspiring. Gerard paints a vision of what the church can be: a community of colour and life and the kind of family we all want to be a part of."
    – **Rob Parsons, Chairman and Founder, Care for the Family**

"Gerard has painted a picture of what it means to be the church of God that will be appreciated for years to come."
    – **Roger Sutton, faith and community leader**

"Gerard paints four memorable word-portraits of a church restored to the chromatic intensity of God's original and brilliant design. Creative, inspirational and eye-opening."
    – **Jeff Fountain, Schuman Centre for European Studies**

"Provocative and prophetic. Gerard reminds us of the mysterious and profound beauty of the local church. A powerful book."
    – **Malcolm Duncan, Minister, Goldhilll Baptist Church**

"Gerard is a creature all too rare in the church – a Leader of Thought. The questions he poses may not be comfortable, but their timeliness and relevance are indisputable. I love this book."
    – **Bev Murrill, Director, Christian Growth International**

"A celebration of church which paints it as vibrant, colourful and actually beautiful."
    – **Martin Young, Minister, Rising Brook Baptist Church**

"A rich, evocative, beautifully written, and heart-expanding exploration of God's purposes for his people, gathering in love and lovingly active out in God's world. Bravo."
    – **Mark Greene, London Institute for Contemporary Christianity**

"Gerard Kelly incites my intrigue, confirms my conviction and bolsters my belief that the church actually is God's brilliant idea for his people and our world."
    – **Russ Rook, Founder, Chapel Street**

"Gerard helps us re-own our puzzling, sometimes frustrating church and see it in all its glorious technicolour. Enjoy!"
    – **Pete Broadbent, Bishop of Willesden**

"Characteristically creative and imaginative… Read it and be envisioned."
    – **Ian Coffey, Director of Leadership Training, Moorlands College**

"Will help our churches make a profound impact within our communities – like a church actually should."
    – **Andrew Marin, author of *Love Is an Orientation***

"Thoughtful and timely… A must read."
    – **Andy Hickford, Senior Minister, Maybridge Community Church**

CHURCH
△CTUALLY

REDISCOVERING THE BRILLIANCE OF GOD'S PLAN

GERARD
KELLY

MONARCH
BOOKS

Oxford, UK & Grand Rapids, Michigan, USA

Published by Monarch Books (an imprint of Lion Hudson plc)
Wilkinson House, Jordan Hill Road, Oxford OX2 8DR, England
email monarch@lionhudson.com; www.lionhudson.com/monarch
and by Elevation (an imprint of the Memralife Group)
Memralife Group, 14 Horsted Square, Uckfield, East Sussex TN22 1QG
Tel: +44 (0)1825 746530; Fax +44 (0)1825 748899;
www.elevationmusic.com

ISBN 978 0 85721 231 3 (print)
ISBN 978 0 85721 285 6 (epub)
ISBN 978 0 85721 284 9 (Kindle)

First edition 2012

Acknowledgments
Unless otherwise stated, Scripture quotations taken from the Holy Bible, New International Version, copyright © 1973, 1978, 1984 by the International Bible Society. Used by permission of Zondervan and Hodder & Stoughton Limited. All rights reserved. The 'NIV' and 'New International Version' trademarks are registered in the United States Patent and Trademark Office by International Bible Society. Use of either trademark requires the permission of International Bible Society. UK trademark number 1448790. Scripture quotations marked NLT are taken from the Holy Bible, New Living Translation, copyright © 1996, 2004, 2007 by Tyndale House Foundation. Used by permission of Tyndale House Publishers, Inc., Carol Stream, Illinois 60188. All rights reserved. Scripture quotations marked Phillips are taken from The New Testament in Modern English, Revised Edition, translated by J.B. Phillips. Copyright © 1958, 1960, 1972 by J.B. Phillips. Reprinted with the permission of Simon & Schuster.

A catalogue record for this book is available from the British Library

For Chrissie and for Anna,
the two women who have most shaped my life;
most taught me the nature of love;
and most empowered me for the journey
of whose fruits this book is just one flavour.

Contents

God's Brilliant Idea #4: "Make Them One!"

Epilogue: The Most Brilliant Idea Ever

Acknowledgments

This book is truly the child of a village, and though the words are mine, the ideas that have shaped them come from many others – even more so the inspiration to write them. I want to especially thank two groups of people.

The Theme Group and Staff Team of Memralife and Spring Harvest have journeyed with this material from its infancy, and have made vital and life-saving changes to its early drafts. Thank you for your friendship, your partnership and your honesty.

The team and trustees of the Bless Network, including the wonderful community now based at Bethanie, have been my extended family for so long that every word of this book reflects, in some measure, their influence. Thank you for being part of the journey. Thank you for being true community.

One person in particular deserves special mention, not least for belonging to both of the above groups. Pete Broadbent, Bishop of Willesden, has been a friend and dialogue partner for many years, and has challenged my thinking on church more often, and more fruitfully, than anyone I know. He is also the source of the wonderful phrase "God's Brilliant Idea", without which this book would be considerably more grey. Thanks, Pete, for the colours you bring to the party.

Introduction:
God's Brilliant Idea

To a lily God is Lagerfeld.
To the birds Raymond Blanc.
To the grass he is Gauguin.
Clothe us, God.
Feed us.
Colour our lives.[1]

The picturesque fishing village of Collioure lies in the extreme south-western corner of France, close to the city of Perpignan and a little over 20 km from the border with Spain. The lumbering Pyrenees mountains finally meet the sea here, creating the two sheltered bays around which the town has grown. These grey-green dinosaurs form a northern backdrop to Collioure but to the south the town opens up to the sparkling waters of the Mediterranean. Brightly painted fishing boats rock gently in the harbour. Mellow sandstone walls under clay tile roofs boast shutters in shades of yellow, green and blue. Pavement cafés, galleries and buskers jointly cater for a year-round flow of tourists.

Well known to the sailors of the Greek and Roman worlds, Collioure later served as the summer home of the kings of Morocco and was a significant lay-over for the knights of the Crusades. But ancient as the town may be, its greatest claim to fame came later – through pilgrims of a very different sort. In the late nineteenth and early twentieth centuries artists from Charles Rennie Mackintosh to Picasso found inspiration in the area's temperate climate and intense southern light. For many years Collioure was a thriving centre of the French art scene.

Two painters in particular, Henri Matisse and André Derain, are associated with the town. In the summer of 1905 the pair produced some 242 canvases here between them: paintings of such vibrant colour and wild brush-strokes that they gave birth to the first significant art movement of the twentieth century. Matisse and Derain excelled in using strident, bright pigments, and when they exhibited their work in Paris an unimpressed critic compared the experience to being "trapped in a cage full of wild animals". From his comment the name *fauves* (literally, "wild animals") was given to the artists, and "Fauvism" was born. The movement was an unapologetic celebration of colour, and the sun-soaked streets and dancing light of a Mediterranean port were the perfect fuel for the journey. "In France there is no sky as blue as the one in Collioure…" Henri Matisse wrote. "I have all the colors of the Mediterranean before me."[2] For the Fauves, colour was the heart of art. The movement was short-lived but was nonetheless both explosive and influential, providing a vital bridge between the Impressionists of the nineteenth century and the new movements of Expressionist and Abstract art that would emerge to dominate the twentieth.

If you visit Collioure today you will find this association celebrated in a unique permanent exhibition, "Le Chemin du Fauvisme" (The Fauvism Path). Reproductions of twenty of the most significant paintings of Matisse and Derain have been framed for display not in a gallery but in the open air – in exactly the places where they were painted.[3] Visitors can take in views almost unchanged since the artists first saw them, at the same time as enjoying the paintings they produced.

To add to this unique experience, Catalan artist Marc André

De Figueres has constructed twelve empty picture frames, each one mounted on a pole and placed close to one of the Fauvist works. Carefully angled to catch the views the artists sought to reproduce, the empty frames challenge the visitor to see what the artist saw while at the same time considering what the artist made of what he saw.

The effect is arresting. *Le Phare de Collioure*,[4] for example, is André Derain's 1905 painting of the town's church, Notre Dame des Anges. A squat stone building surrounded on three sides by water, the church also serves as a lighthouse, marking the entry-way to the safety of the town's harbour. Asked to describe the colours of this ancient building, most visitors would say "beige" or "grey". On a good day, under the generous southern sun, we might call it golden. But Derain's painting knows no such limitations: it is an explosion of colour. Bold strokes of red, orange and yellow define the walls against the impossible blue of the sea. The rocky foundations of the church are stark in green, black and blue. The windows, in shadow, are not just dark but jet black, emphasizing by contrast the riot of colour outside.

Contemporary visitors to Collioure, viewing this ancient building through Figueres' golden frame, cannot help but compare their own impoverished vision with the colour and life that Derain saw. The very contrast challenges them to consider the "truths" that the artist has seen and they have not. When the Mediterranean sun hits an old stone wall, all those colours are there. The sea can seem impossibly blue on such a day. Stones can shimmer with colour and life. Shadows are deeper and darker where the sun is brighter. The eye of the artist has not seen things that are not there, but has seen more completely what is there already. Artists, like prophets, are not looking at a world no one else can see; they are looking upon what everyone else sees but seeing it differently. Where we see shades of grey, a great artist might see explosions of colour.

When I visited Collioure late in 2008 I was deeply struck by the "Chemin du Fauvism" exhibition. Like thousands of tourists before, I stood looking at a grey church through an empty golden frame and was convicted of my own lack of vision and imagination. What would it take, I wondered, for me to see the colours a great artist might see? What courage would I need to celebrate what I saw, even as others around me, more rationally defined and fearing excess, named me wild?

A student more of mission than of art, more familiar with churches than galleries, I accepted this rebuke at the very heart of my faith. I understood that here was a metaphor that made sense of many of the unnamed feelings I had lived with, and recognized in others, for many years. Standing in the stark light of this contrast – the experience of looking simultaneously at a dull, grey building and at the carnival of colour an artist has seen in it – I was forced to consider my own misgivings about the way I have lived out my faith, and the way I see it widely being lived.

This has become a vital metaphor to me in recent years as I have wrestled with the loss of colour that so many people describe in their experience of the Christian faith. How has a movement that began as an explosion of colour and life become so bland – so grey – in our experience?

It would be gratifying to be able to dismiss this as a trivial question, but history does not allow us to do so. In the century since Derain and Matisse first painted in Collioure, tens of millions of people have walked away from commitment to the Christian churches of the West. In the European context, the sociologist Grace Davie describes this change as the end of church membership "by obligation". She suggests that it is not only the most significant shift on the religious landscape of Europe in recent years, but the single most significant shift in European society as a whole. A continent that once had church and the experience of church at the very heart of its life and culture now does not. Whatever hold the Christian story once had on the European imagination, it is losing or has lost. And those walking away from faith often experience their journey as a kind of liberation. Looking back over their shoulder to see what they have left behind, they see grey. Old buildings; empty creeds; bland faith. What they do not see is colour and life.

And yet the church is, in its origins, God's brilliant idea. It is his plan; the Creator's way of reaching and redeeming his creation. It is a sparkling idea, a concept radiant with light and joy. Words like "brilliant", "bright" and "beautiful" can legitimately be used to describe it. But such words sound hollow, all too often, when applied to our experience of church. Those who have left don't hesitate to express the dullness of their view of church. Those left behind are more circumspect, perhaps, trying hard to emphasize the positive. But many of us, deep inside, know it to be true. Church has become, for us, grey. What happened to the fountain of colour God switched on at Pentecost? Where did the explosion of joy go? How did a movement of life and exuberance become, for so many, a source of greyness in our world?

Church Actually is an attempt to look honestly at these questions and to recover a picture of the church alive with colour; pulsing with life; explosive with joy. It is a journey into the mission of God, to seek out lost colours and recover vibrant vision. Can we break out of the greyness of our church experience to discover the riot of colour God intended? Is there a route back to the brilliance of God's plan? Like Mark Figueres with his empty frames, I want to ask you, "What do you see?" and challenge you, perhaps, to see more.

When we came to these questions in the planning of Spring Harvest 2012, we identified four specific "brilliant ideas" that create the framework of the New Testament church: four essential elements of the church's identity and purpose. If the church were a kitchen table, these would be the four legs. They hold the vision together, calling us to a life lived in full colour.

Our purpose here is to spend time exploring each of these four in a series of short chapters, allowing you to read one a day over twenty-one days, or to just keep reading until you're done. For each we will ask what the Bible tells us about the brilliance of God's plan for the church, and what it might take to recover that brilliance in our own generation. Each of the four brilliant ideas points towards two tasks for the church: areas of activity or ministry that allow God's plan to move forward. By giving attention to the eight tasks that emerge in due course from our journey, we believe that it is possible to recover the brilliance of God's plan: to move towards expressions of church that are, in the words of missiologist Lesslie Newbigin, "an explosion of joy in their community".

The four brilliant ideas are:

God's brilliant idea #1:
"Shine through them"

The most rudimentary definition of the church is "the people of God": a collective noun represented in the New Testament by the Greek term *ekklesia*. The church exists because God has committed himself to work through people. This is the fulfilment of the Creator's long-held intention to shine wisdom through his human creatures into the world he has made. We will explore this as a *prismatic* plan: the many colours of God's wisdom displayed through redeemed human lives. This is the human-centredness of God's plan: it is a plan that works through people. We will assert that the church is truly fulfilling this plan when it serves to equip God's people for the full diversity of their callings and vocations. What does it take to shine God's light into every corner of our culture?

God's brilliant idea #2:
"Give them power"

A second biblical metaphor for the church is "the community of the Spirit": a human community *indwelt* by the Holy Spirit. This is a dynamic expression of God's promise to live with and within his people. We will examine the *charismystic* nature of this reality, placing at the very heart of church experience a dynamic relationship with the Spirit of God. We will see that because it is a Spirit-driven movement, the church is always both established and emerging, taking shape around God's mission in the world. We are called to be both rooted and booted. We will celebrate God as the gift-giver, and see that spiritual formation, the forming of the character of Christ in us by the Spirit, is key to God's mission in the world. What is God doing *in us* that will empower and resource what he plans to do *through us*?

God's brilliant idea #3:
"Help them love"

The third brilliant idea, perhaps the New Testament's most dramatic metaphor for the church, is "the body of Christ". As individuals are drawn together into this one body, they become the new dispersed presence of the risen Jesus in the world, the new carriers of his words and works. We will examine the church's call to be a *transformant* task force, changing the world through acts of love and service. We will ask whether the recovery of servant love as the very mark of the church might not lead to a renewal of its life and mission, asserting that God's kingdom runs on *meekonomics* – the subverting of power and wealth that brings the margins to the centre. How might a tidal wave of small acts of love change the direction of our over-consuming culture? What does it mean for us to incarnate anew the very life of Christ?

God's brilliant idea #4:
"Make them one"

Lastly, we will discover the New Testament's future-focused vision of the church as the "bride of Christ", a body resplendent with beauty reflecting the colours and contributions of every culture on the planet. We will examine the *metanational* movement that the church has become as the seeds of God's story are sown into ever new people groups and languages, and ask how this beauty can be reflected in our life and worship. Might the Bible's story of reconciled relationships be the key our culture is searching for, to form all-age, every-culture community? Is there a vision for the church in which every human story finds meaning; a table to which all are invited? We will assert that God's story is *translatable*, making itself available to every human culture and language. What does it mean to truly celebrate diversity?

God's imagineers

Having explored these four "brilliant ideas", we will see how they come together to support the kitchen table that is the kingdom of God. This is the ultimate vision, and the ultimate task of the church: to announce the coming of God's kingdom. Our life of liturgy and prayer; our rhythms of gathering and dispersal; our attention to worship and discipleship – all these come together in the one cry, "Let your kingdom come, and your will be done, on earth as it is in heaven..." We will assert the radical polarity of this prayer, representing a movement not from earth to heaven but from heaven to earth. We will ask what the kingdom looks like, and assert the church's ultimate and most pressing task: to imagine an answer.

Story wars

The significance of these four "brilliant ideas" and of the eight tasks they point us towards does not arise purely and simply because they are present in the Bible. It arises also from their relevance to our present situation. They are not a description of the church as it is theoretically described, but as it is actually called to be.

As such they are a response to the very real crisis in which the Western church finds itself. A culture is shaped by hope and aspiration, defined by the stories it tells of itself, and the West has walked away from the church because the church's narrative no longer inspires. A monochrome story fails to catch the breath of those who hear it. For millions of people across Europe the Christian churches have been archived in memory and history: they form part of our past but not of our future and have no power to fuel our dreams today.

No culture on earth has been post-Christian in quite the way Europe is. We have been through the years of Christendom and come out the other side. Contemporary Christians are minoritized and marginalized, small in number and forced to the edges of the culture. The story that shaped the art and institutions of the West over centuries no longer does so. The Christian adventure has lost its capacity to inspire the heart and ignite the human imagination. For some, this is cause for great rejoicing, as the era of Christendom – a world-dominating Eurocentric faith marrying political and spiritual powers – is once and for all declared dead.

But leaving behind the baggage of an imperial faith is one thing. Leaving behind the very story that has shaped us is a deeper loss altogether. Where we go next has global ramifications. "We're fighting a new kind of war: a Story War", Leonard Sweet has suggested. "Who ultimately wins? The one who out-narrates the opposition, who tells the better story."[5]

Is there a faith-story to inspire again the hearts and minds of the West? Can we escape the monochrome narratives of modernity to recover the richer colours of God's story? To do so will require us to confront three questions currently surfacing in the emerging generations.

No automatic transmission

The first is the vital question of faith transmission.

Passing on the faith is not an option, it is a biblical imperative. Psalm 78 expresses this in the ancient commitment to "tell the next generation about the glorious deeds of the Lord".[6]

For me, this has meant wrestling over three decades with the challenge of evangelism and youth ministry in Europe. Living and working in the UK, France and the Netherlands and engaging with local churches across Europe, I have seen at first hand the uncontrolled "spillage" of faith, as congregation after congregation, denomination after denomination, singularly fails to capture the imagination of the rising generations. Youth ministry is not only about young people, it is about the future of the church; about the transmission of a faith that, without radical change, will die with the current generation. The need to rediscover the brilliance of God's plan for the church becomes urgent when set against the needs of faith transmission. Unless we find again a full-colour vision of God's church we will lose, again and again, the hearts and allegiance of God's children.

Time to go vs. status quo

The second question is that of the missional church.

For many in the rising generations this question, of the recovery of a truly missional understanding of the life of faith, has become a make-or-break issue. Our young leaders are asking not just that the church should "do" mission, as if programmes and activities could fill the void, but that the church should "be" missional, to its very core: calibrated not to service its members but to serve a world in need.

This quest has found expression in recent years in a whole range of experiments loosely collected under the banner of "emerging church" or "alternative worship" and flowing into mainline denominations in movements such as Fresh Expressions. The missional movement seeks to turn the church away from its inward-focused and maintenance-based agenda to an outward-looking perspective; fostering engagement with the wider culture and a genuine encounter with unchurched and de-churched populations.

But this is a movement in its early stages, and a minority one at that. It is still not clear whether the new missional churches have the capacity to displace outmoded models of church or popular conceptions of the faith. For every book or resource representing the longing for a more missional church there are hundreds, if not thousands, that do not: and the average church experience – for visitors and for adherents – remains tragically unmoving. There is a deathly sense of "business as usual" hanging over much of the Christian world, especially in resources that are produced not for missional specialists but for the "ordinary" Christian. Many of those seeking a deeper missional understanding of the church share a feeling – a deep-down hunch articulated in many different ways but remarkably consistent across the divergent cultures and denominations of the West – that there is something dangerously wrong in the loss of contact between church and culture.

If our churches are ever to be vibrant and healthy again they will need to recover their dynamic dialogue with their host cultures. Inward-looking reflections will not make the cut – it will be at the edges of the church, where the life of faith meets the wider life of society, that healing will be found. What resources will help us find once again, at the meeting-points of church and culture, the energy of a missional faith? Can we move from doing mission as an application of our creeds to living mission as the essence of our faith? What dreams do we need to dream to fund our greater engagement with God's mission in the world?

Shall we gather?

The third question that confronts us is just what the role should be, in our missional adventure, of the gathered and organized expression of church: that aspect of the church to which the adjective "institutional" is most often applied.

Contemporary students of mission are seeing increasingly that the church functions in both a gathered and a dispersed mode, and that it is in dispersal that the most effective mission takes place. They are learning to question the overemphasis, in the Christendom era, on gathering. They wonder if our highly organized, hierarchical and bureaucratic churches might not have become too heavy, too solid for the challenges of mission in a liquid culture. Might we not be better served, they ask, by a de-centred, grassroots movement networking together small and diverse gatherings of Christ-followers? Can't we make everything small and lo-fi, with flat, leaderless structures and organic and anarchic programmes?

Our current models of church have an inbuilt bias towards gathering, and much of our business is to do with community-building and personal growth. Many of the structures and programmes of our churches, from the recruitment and training of clergy to the planning of services and events, are calibrated towards this inward focus. There is a sense in which this emphasis on gathering is a hangover from the Christendom era, when belonging to the assembly of the church was fundamental to social identity: as vital as having an internet connection is today. Physical gathering was the only means by which belonging could be measured, and those in leadership of gathered churches were the unchallenged gatekeepers of salvation.

Such assumptions are being challenged and for the most part abandoned in a culture in which "assembly" is no longer a necessary measure of adherence. But there is another sense in which the instinct to gather, and by implication to organize, is intrinsic to the nature of church: the forming of church is by definition the forming of a new community.

From its very inception the church has been the product of twin forces: the outward movement of the mission of God and the inward gathering of the people of God. There is a centrifugal force throwing the community into mission; looking outwards; seeking a life of adventure and incarnation at the growing edges of the faith. But there is an equal and opposite centripetal force calling the church together: focusing inwards; looking to the strength and solidity of community. The emphasis of the New Testament points both inwards to the health and strength of the community and its members, and outwards to engagement with those beyond the church's walls. The two directions are both present – and both ask for an investment of energy and resources. The inward invitation and outward thrust of the church are the source of its very life.

The most eager advocates of a missional recalibration seem at times to be calling for the complete abandonment of the inward thrust, as if the outward call of mission can only be recovered through a wholesale turnaround. More conservative leaders – raised on the call to shepherd God's people; concerned with the in-gathering and formation of disciples – will tend to reject such a call out of hand, knowing that this inward-call is a necessary and significant part of what we are as people of faith. It seems that we are being asked to choose between inward focus and outward flow, between gathering and dispersal. This feels dangerously close to asking a dying patient if he would prefer to breathe in or breathe out. We can and must do both.

How much of the fact that we gather and our patterns of gathering is intrinsic to the nature of church, and how much of it is Christendom holding on to us? Much has been written on this subject in recent years – more deeply and eloquently than is possible here[7] – but the result for some has been an unhealthy identification of the "gathered" church as an exclusively Christendom model and the "dispersed" or "incarnational" church as the only viable missional alternative – as if only dissolution can save us.[8]

For my own part, I am not convinced by this case. The church that gave birth to Western civilization; that ushered in the Christendom era; that is now so fiercely in decline, was itself born in the outward thrust of the mission of God. Jesus is sent by the Father and sends his followers likewise. The Holy Spirit is sent from heaven to fall upon the church and to flow with them in an outward arc from Jerusalem to the ends of the earth. But wherever this outward-flowing movement interfaces with human culture, the church comes into being. Community is created and with community comes organization and leadership; plans and strategies and budgets; conflicts and divisions and political processes. The "sending-out" movement of God's mission creates the "drawing-in" movement of the church. As a friend recently commented on Twitter, God sends to gather and gathers to send.

I find myself asking if a more nuanced process of change might not be possible, charting a course from where we are now to where we need to be without losing the beauty and significance of church as we have known it. The central question for me is not "Should the church be gathered or dispersed?" but rather, "How does the gathered expression of church resource its missional dispersion?"

In *Get a Grip on the Future*, published in 1998,[9] I explored the changing face of Western culture and the potential for mission to adapt to a post-industrial, post-literate, post-modern, post-imperial and post-Christian future. Since then I have engaged in conversation and dialogue with many key thinkers in the "emergent" and "missional" movements, while at the same time, through the Bless Network, encouraging young people to engage in acts of missional service with established denominations alongside existing, mainstream congregations. *Church Actually* is an attempt to take this twin commitment further, and to ask how the gathered church can once more take its place at the very heart of God's mission in the world. How can the church be at the centre of the action without becoming the centre of attention? How can it harness the resources of the people of God for the sake of mission without drawing those resources to itself? Can we unite for liquidity without creating a deathly solidity?

These three questions – of the transmission of faith in the cultures of the West, of the recovery of a truly missional church and of the bringing together of gathered and dispersed models of mission – have challenged my thinking over thirty years of mission and given rise to the model of faith here presented as *Church Actually* – a model of faith and mission for the twenty-first century that breathes both out and in; that is unashamedly attractional and passionately incarnational; that delights to be gathered and longs to be dispersed; that is organizationally strong but hugely equipping of its individual members; that has immense strength at its centre and unfettered openness at its edge. I want to suggest that in our quest for such a church there are colours we will need to recover; wavelengths of God's mission to which we have perhaps become blind.

It is significant that science, and not aesthetics alone, played a part in shaping the work of the Fauvists and the colour-revolution they gladly joined. Their work was, in part, a response to changes in their cultural landscape.

In the closing years of the nineteenth century and the early years of the twentieth, two areas of research were moving ahead at such a pace as to make new experiments in art not only possible but inevitable. The first was the development of photography and the associated experimentation in the behaviour of light. Early discoveries in photographic processing showed as never before the relationship between sight and light and revealed much that had never before been so fully understood. This led to discoveries about refraction and the nature of colour that gave avant-garde artists new confidence in their experimentation. They were freed to "see" more than they had ever seen before, understanding that the light pouring into their eyes carried many more colours than their rational minds had previously acknowledged.

In parallel to this, developments in the manufacture and import of pigments were offering to the painter unprecedented power to reproduce the colours he was seeing. Year by year new pigments became available or affordable, and each one added to the artist's armoury. The Impressionists, most notably Monet, were the first to take advantage of these developments and break into new areas of experimentation with colour. The journey was taken further by the post-Impressionists and by Seurat and the Pointillists – who painted by applying thousands of tiny dots of disparate colours – until the baton was passed to the Fauvists and beyond.

All in all, the art world of the late nineteenth and early twentieth centuries was a carnival of colour: a global celebration of polychromatic light. As representatives of this period, Matisse and Derain, honoured to this day in the town of Collioure, stand as ambassadors of colour – prophets of a technicolour future. The wildness of their paintings should not be dismissed as naive and over-imaginative playfulness: it is underpinned by a deep and essentially scientific interaction with colour. The Fauves are not Surrealists. They are not trying to tell us what they have dreamed or imagined. They are trying to tell us what they see. Colour, for them, is reality. It is our paler, more monochrome view that is imagined, imposed on our vision by a cold rationalism that insists on informing us that stone "is" grey. Derain and Matisse want to break open the limited and limiting perceptions that dull our senses. They are artists engaging with a changing world. They want to free us to see all the colours light has for us.

Can you hear the Holy Spirit, through them, calling you to a fuller vision of the church?

God's Brilliant Idea #1:
"Shine Through Them!"

The church as a prismatic people

pris·mat·ic (prĭz-măt′ĭk)
also **pris·mat·i·cal** (-ĭ-kəl)
Adjective: of, relating to, resembling, or being a prism. Formed by refraction of light through a prism. Used of a spectrum of light. Brilliantly coloured; iridescent.

pris·mat·ic church (prĭz-măt′ĭk chûrch)
Noun: all the colours of God's wisdom through all the callings of God's people to every corner of God's world.

Assembly Lines

From the start the biblical narrative asserts that God is not alone,
and neither should humans be. We are relational creatures reflecting
our relational creator. The call to form community arises directly and
specifically from the nature of God as Trinity.[1]

Key Text: Acts 19:32

The assembly was in confusion: Some were shouting one thing, some
another. Most of the people did not even know why they were there.[2]

Abstract

**At its simplest, church is the assembly of God's people – the
collective noun of which "disciple" is the singular form. But
it is much more than that. It is the focus of God's joy; the new
community made possible in Christ, in which we find out what it
means to be human.**

The gathering described in Acts 19 is rowdy, noisy and confusing.

A group of citizens, angry at the disruption Paul and his travelling team have brought to Ephesus, call an emergency town meeting to discuss what should be done. Passers-by are drawn into the crowd. Tempers flare and temperatures rise.

In the end, fearing a riot, the town clerk dismisses the assembly and disperses the crowd. And the word that is used throughout the passage to describe the assembly is *ekklesia* – later adopted as the New Testament's most common word for "church". Like citizens coming together to discuss their concerns for their city, an *ekklesia* is a gathering of people who share a particular identity and unite around common concerns.

The base word for church in the New Testament is, in effect, "assembly". At its simplest level, before history added layers of hierarchy, varieties of denominations and the unbearable weight of a million expectations, "church" meant in essence "Christians together". It is the collective noun of the singular "disciple". To acknowledge the simplicity of this definition does not mean that we are calling into question all that history has added – much of this is good and valuable. But it does mean acknowledging that at its heart the church is a simple construct. It is what happens when believers journey together. I am a disciple of Christ. We are the church of Christ. Before it is about anything else, the church is about people.

Buried in the simplicity of this construct is a calling of immense depth. God calls us to respond to his love and grace not only as individuals, but as part of a body. For the evangelists of the New Testament, "coming to faith" and "joining the church" were synonymous. Baptism was the symbol both of personal salvation and of initiation into the community of faith. There was no discipleship that did not have a collective and corporate expression. The "I" of faith confession was linked to the "we" of credal unity. Believing and belonging were the two indivisible sides of the one coin of faith.

This sense of corporate or collective identity was immediately apparent to the first Jewish Christians, because they knew that *ekklesia* was also used in the Greek translation of the Old Testament to describe the congregation or assembly of the Hebrew slaves as they crossed the desert.[3] The church is the people of God, drawn together in the shared experience of liberation, journeying towards the shared inheritance of the promised land. As Israel is the people of God in the desert, so the church is the people of God in the world today. Whether our experience is of exodus or of exile, we are God's people and he journeys with us.

It is this common purpose that gives us common cause,

and draws us into commitment. If you stand at a bus stop early in the morning, there is little or no pressure to talk to your fellow-travellers. There is no certainty that they will catch the same bus as you, and even if they do they will take a different seat, read a different book and in all likelihood get off at a different stop. They may even wear white ear-phones to let you know of their need for isolation. But if you are waiting for a bus that will take you to a sports match, and those at the stop are your fellow team-members, and the outcome of the match will decide if your club gets promoted or not... you can bet that you will talk to each other. You have a shared goal, a task to perform, and being in relationship is a big part of performing it well.

The second bus stop is a better image of the church than the first, even though those at it may seem like strangers to us. Strangers or not, we have shared goals, and a task to fulfil. We are called, together, to build a community that touches the world. We are carriers of a message and a mandate that has life-changing implications. And step one of the instructions left to us is "talk to each other".

The corporate and collective nature of God's plan means that we are called to this model whether it appeals to us or not. To be an authentic follower of Christ in the world, I must at some level come to terms with others who have made the same choice. I am called not only to follow but to find fellow followers. For some this is a challenge, because their experience of church is a little too literally like the Acts 19 *ekklesia*, where some shout one thing, some another, and most of the people don't even know why they are there. They see dullness and disunity, strife and small-mindedness, and they say, "No, thank you." They wonder, "Can't I follow Christ alone?" Such a question would have been strange to the ears of a New Testament Christian, because the statement "I want to believe" carried within itself the statement "I want to belong". To be born into faith was to be born into family, into community. But we struggle today because we have separated the notion of believing – a private and personal decision – from that of belonging – a separate and optional choice.

Can we recover the corporate and collective dimension of our faith-confession? Can we look at our fellow-believers not simply as other people who happen to be at the same bus stop as us, but as our team-mates, people we are called to work and play with, whose interactions with us may just make the difference between winning and losing? Recovering a sense of the corporate and collective call of the church, rediscovering reasons to journey together, is vital to the re-imagining of faith in the twenty-first century. If we let individual achievement – my gifts; my goals; my glory – take the place of a shared, united and jointly held vision, we will have lost a vital element of New Testament faith. We will be thin where we should be robust; weak where we should be strong; impoverished where we should be rich. In the theology of the Orthodox churches, we would in this situation be less than fully human: *ekklesia* does not simply gather us, it completes us. The Orthodox theologian Zizioulas describes this as "the ecclesiological significance of the person", and distinguishes it from "our merely biological existence in which we exist as disconnected individuals". For Zizioulas, the belonging the church makes possible substantially adds to our existence as individuals. "In the church we are made persons; persons in communion. Through baptism and faith, biological existence gives way to existence in koinonia."[4]

The church, then, is not simply an accident of mission, nor a mere function of faith. It is the expression of the new humanity made possible in Christ; the revealing of the new human community to which all are offered access. If we are to recover a full-colour picture of God's plans for the world, we're going to need to fall in love again with his brilliant idea, the church.

Think About It: Restore

In 2010 a group of us worked together on a Europe-wide project called "Restore".[5] A call to the people of God to pray for the continent of Europe, Restore took a programme of worship, poetry and prayer to four ancient churches across Europe – three of them cathedrals – in Lincoln, Lisieux, Florence and Prague. Standing in the echoing emptiness of these fortresses of faith, we dared to believe that among the ruins of a religion in decline God can rebuild his church. The call is vital, as alternative worldviews threaten to engulf whole populations. The call is deep, as a faith buried in the centuries of Europe's history seeks to find its voice again. The call is urgent, as a new generation grow up not knowing of the treasures their parents have so thoughtlessly squandered.

This poem formed part of the evening. It is a cry to God for the restoration of his church in Europe. Can you echo its cry in your own heart?

Restore

Where our walls are broken down
Rebuild us God
Where streets are neither safe nor sound
Redeem

Rekindle
Fires of once strong praise
Resound your joys
In tone and phrase
From ancient stones of walls
Once raised for you

Where feelings fail
For want of fuel
Ignite renewal, reanimate
Where hearts won't start
Where your call has stalled
Resuscitate, reactivate,
Reload, rewire, recreate
Re-cut us as a jewel
To catch your light

Return, Messiah King
Let these stones sing
Restore, strong son of love
Let these bones live
Rework the threads of tangled lives
Re-weave them into grace
Redress disgrace
Reassemble the dismembered
May we remember
Who we are

Repossess our peeling planet
God of rescue and repair
Renovate, regenerate
Resolve disease
Replace despair
Reconstruct, reconstitute
Recalibrate, reframe us
Reclaim us God of lost and found
In love re-ground
In grace rename us

Return, Messiah King
Let these stones sing
Restore, strong son of love
Let these bones live
Rework the threads of tangled lives
Re-weave them into grace
Redress disgrace
Reassemble the dismembered
May we remember
Who we are[6]

Prismatic People

The church is not a random collection of people: it is people brought together for a purpose. God's plan for the church is to "shine" his wisdom through all those who follow Christ. God wants to shine through people, and the process by which he does this is called "church".[1]

Key Text: Ephesians 3:10

His intent was that now, through the church, the manifold wisdom of God should be made known to the rulers and authorities in the heavenly realms.[2]

Abstract

It is not only in the church that God wants to shine his light, it is also through the church. The *ekklesia*, gathering together all those who have chosen to connect with God in Christ, becomes the "people movement" through which God chooses to make his character and wisdom known.

Paul was not the founder of the Christian church, nor was he the first of its leaders, but more than anyone he watched over its expansion and growth and worked tirelessly to ensure that it stayed healthy. As the church spread out from Jerusalem, springing up in new communities wherever the seed of the Christian story found fertile soil, Paul formed close bonds with many of the faith's new leaders. When the river of Christian mission burst the banks of Judaism, and Greek and Roman cultures began to host their own Bible clubs, he became a go-between. He built strong friendships with the emerging leaders of the new missional churches, but he also stayed in touch with the Jerusalem apostles, acknowledging their authority and referring back to them when questions arose.

It was to Paul, more than to anyone, that the task fell of shaping and structuring the emerging missional churches of Asia Minor. Time and again he encountered the Holy Spirit at work in the diverse destinations of his journeys, and time and again he saw a church come into being as a result.

In his letter to the Ephesian Christians, the apostle distils the wisdom and experience of decades of such encounters to capture a vision for the church. Particularly in chapters 3 and 4, he outlines an approach to the new community of faith that places the church at the very centre of a new human adventure. The *ekklesia* is the gathering of human beings who have chosen, in Christ, to return to their God-appointed place as the light-bearers of the created world. Salvation is a new way to be human. In Ephesians 3:10 Paul places the church at the very centre of God's purposes, setting its edges as far as possible in the outward thrust of mission:

> *His intent was that now, through the church, the manifold wisdom of God should be made known to the rulers and authorities in the heavenly realms, according to his eternal purpose that he accomplished in Christ Jesus our Lord.*[3]

A traditional reading of this verse has God's wisdom as "many-coloured". This is a vision of the church as prismatic by its very nature. Even at a time before prismatic light was understood, Paul understood the notion of something pure and blended (the wisdom of God) being broken out, somehow, into its constituent parts. The pure white light of God's wisdom hits the community of faith and breaks into its many colours, reaching to the very heavens with its light. God intends that all the colours of his wisdom should be seen in the created world

– and his chosen method of making them visible is refraction: specifically refraction through human agency.

The community of faith is the lens through which God's light shines out into the world. The church is prismatic not only in the sense that it bears and expresses the many colours of God's wisdom, but also in the sense that it is itself the prism. The God who has always been committed to shining light through humanity is now doing so through a new network of redeemed human beings, collectively called "the church".

These assertions are important for a number of reasons but none more so than that they capture the vital relationship between the church and God's mission in the world. Paul locates the church at the very centre of God's purposes. That which God has always wanted to do, his "intent", he is now able to do through the *ekklesia*. The *ekklesia* comes into being through mission – Paul has seen churches emerge in Jewish, Greek, Roman and pagan settings – but mission then comes to life through the *ekklesia*. God is doing remarkable things in the church – its very community reflects his grace and character – but that is not in itself enough. He also wants to do remarkable things through the church. The church is a community born with a purpose: it is missional by nature, and it is in the discovery of God-given purposes – in the embracing of its missional calling – that the church comes closest to knowing and declaring its identity.

The church, then, is the means by which God is now working to achieve the goal he has had from the beginning, which is to pour wisdom into the creation through his human representatives. Paul's knowledge of the Jewish Scriptures is unparalleled. The implication here is that the "cultural mandate" of Genesis 1:26–28 – God's initial declaration of intent for Adam and Eve – is rolled into this new calling of the church. It is in the church that God is now seeking the earthly representatives that Adam and Eve so dramatically failed to be.

Christian environmentalists have recently taken to calling the mandate given to Adam and Eve – the command to care for and "husband" the earth – the "First Commission", a valuable reminder that before there was ever a "Great Commission" God had already called human beings to engagement in his purposes. Jesus' own reaffirmation of that same call in Matthew 5 is also echoed in Ephesians 3:10. Eugene Peterson's poetic translation reads:

You're here to be salt-seasoning that brings out the God-flavors of this Earth... You're here to be light, bringing out the God-colors in the world.[4]

Paul's choice of the Jewish category of "wisdom" in Ephesians 3:10 to capture this process is important. Today's churches tend to be more concerned about the church displaying "truth" or "love", but the choice is deliberate. "Wisdom" in the Hebrew worldview is the application of God's truth to everyday life. It is by God's wisdom that a farmer knows when to sow and when to reap, and how to grind different grains.[5] Wisdom addresses commerce and culture, relationships, art, sport, science. It is the interaction of God's truth with human culture.

In redeemed humanity, brought together as "church", God has created a process – a mechanism – by which the mandate given to Adam can be fulfilled. He has set in place a new movement of representatives, and a means to extend that movement to the very ends of the earth, touching every level and expression of culture. Paul, the Jewish scholar, is making a remarkable claim in Ephesians 3:10. He wraps up his whole understanding of the "intentions of God" – everything he has ever believed God was seeking to do through the Jewish nation; everything that was given to Adam to do, and subsequently to Abraham and Joseph and Moses, to David and all who came

after him – and asserts that these intentions are now vested in the church.

What God has always been seeking to do, he now does through the church. What God has always wanted for the world, he now wants through the church. What God has always longed to pour out on the world, he will now pour out through the movement called the church.

Our participation in this movement will be greatly advanced if we can begin to understand two concepts crucial to the New Testament – mission and the kingdom of God.

Think About It: "Tell it in Colour"

Tell it in Colour is a Belfast-based website committed to publishing the "good news" stories that are all around the city. For years Belfast has been associated with "the troubles" and the news has been of violence and hatred. www.tellitincolour.com responds not by complaining about the darkness but by loving the light – a great example of prismatic mission in action...

The King's Dome

The Creator has always looked for people who through intimacy and obedience will reflect his character, to bring out "the God-flavours" and "the God-colours" of the world. The New Testament speaks of what God wants to do in people, but also of what he longs to do through people. God's plan has always been to shine through people and since the life, death, resurrection and ascension of Jesus the movement that makes God's shining possible is called "church".[1]

Key Text: Matthew 11:12

The kingdom of heaven has been forcefully advancing, and forceful men lay hold of it...[2]

Abstract

The concepts of church, mission and kingdom all belong together. Church as the community of God's purposes, the kingdom as the goal of God's purposes and mission as the bridge between the two.

Central to Paul's description of the church in Ephesians 3 is the idea that while God is at work within the church, his goal is to achieve something beyond the church – so far beyond, in fact, that the very courts of heaven are affected.

Taking the New Testament as a whole, it is clear that this "something" is the kingdom of God or, as described in Matthew's gospel, the kingdom of heaven. This kingdom, essentially the condition within which the will of God is done "on earth as in heaven", is the goal to which the church is called. As Jurgen Moltmann has written, "the mission of the church is not to spread the church but to spread the kingdom".[3] Understanding what the kingdom is, and how the church relates to it, will enable us to develop an understanding of mission that is colourful, robust and compelling, and frees us from the twin traps of narrow conversionism on the one hand and bland liberalism on the other.

Our problem is that we tend to interpret mission in one of these ways. In the first, mission is entirely and exclusively to do with persuading other people to become Christians. Whether we call it evangelism, outreach or faith-sharing, it has the same goal: the numerical growth of the church, as individuals make the decision to convert. Recruitment becomes the overarching purpose of the church, and when we ask what we are recruiting people to do, the answer comes back, "To recruit others!" In this model the only growth that counts is numerical growth, and the sole focus of the kingdom is the conversion of the individual: not to a life of purpose and beauty, but to a life of converting others. At best this reduces the biblical vision of the kingdom to the narrow scope of individual salvation. At worst, it turns the whole enterprise into a pyramid selling scheme: an Amway model that our friends and neighbours are quite right to steer clear of.

The conversionist approach takes a vital and important element of mission, and tries to make it the whole deal. Faith formation must be part of mission. If the church is the means by which the kingdom comes, then the growth of the church, by definition, offers opportunities for the growth of the kingdom. Every life surrendered to the purposes of God is a further opportunity for his glory to be seen. But conversionism alone is not enough, just as the raw decision to follow Christ is not enough to sustain a lifelong, life-transforming faith. Beyond the decision there is discipleship, and discipleship is all about the kingdom of God.

The alternative view is that everything we do is mission.

God loves us and everything we do under the benevolent dome of his love is mission. Whether or not people become Christians. Whether or not the church grows. Whether or not we see measurable, accountable change. It's all mission because it all matters and God sees and knows it all. The kingdom fades into a mildly improved version of what we already know, and everything we already do is baptized by our "missional" intent. This is not unlike the prayer meeting where we forget to pray, gossip instead and then close by saying, "God, you have heard every word of our conversation…" As if talking becomes prayer just because we say so. But if all our words are prayers, prayer ceases to exist as any kind of meaningful exercise. And if everything is mission, mission disappears.

With this approach mission loses all shape. If we can't say that an activity is explicitly not missional, then there is nothing to be gained from saying that another activity is. Jesus, Mahatma Gandhi and the team from *Extreme Home Makeover* blend together into a beige-coloured stream of niceness, and there is no sense in which a biblically informed cultural engagement can be distinguished from any other.

In between these two views there is a third option, articulated in the New Testament and offered as the church's job description. In this view, God has established the church as the community in whom his intentions will be vested. He calls that community to work and pray for a very specific goal: the coming of his kingdom. This is further defined as the condition in which God's will is done on earth. The mission of God is for the will of God to be done, and our participation in that process is our missional calling. Anything, in this view, that moves some aspect of the created order from rebellion to obedience, from God's will not being done to God's will being done, is missional.

Further, Paul helps us to see this in specifically ecclesial terms. Because God has chosen to bring the kingdom by shining his wisdom through the church, we can further define our own missional participation in God's purposes; to say that any activity in which God's wisdom, shining through God's people, results in God's will being done where it wasn't before, is a missional activity. Mission cannot simply be a mindless, undiscerning embracing of culture in all its forms: rather it is a determination, in every expression of culture and at every level of society, to see the will of God done. This model includes evangelism and faith-formation, because these activities, by definition, call for a movement from rebellion to obedience. Evangelistic mission is constructed on the notion of the will of God being done, where it has not been done before, in the life of an individual or group. The evangelists can take their stand, alongside others in the church, as kingdom-builders.

But they cannot claim to be the only ones. The kingdom also includes justice in commerce; beauty in art; an end to addiction and pornography. It leads to swords being remodelled as ploughshares, and lions meekly sleeping next to lambs. It involves the hungry being fed and the naked clothed. It includes, as we will see in a later chapter, transformation in the personal, relational, social and global dimensions. It includes every kind of life-improvement where that life-improvement comes about because the wisdom of God is poured into and through the people of God. Other changes may take place in our world, and be laudable: but they are not missional unless this last criterion is included. Mission is the will of God being done because of the light he shines through his people.

To return to Eugene Peterson's beautiful rendition of Matthew 5, we can perhaps say that mission takes place wherever God's people bring out the God-flavours of the world; wherever the light shining through them brings out the God-colours. Mission is colour in a monochrome world. It is shape in the world of the flat. It is the declaration and delivery of the Creator's intentions.

I was once told by a good friend who is a committed Methodist, and no fan of John Calvin, that "no significant mission had taken place" in the 200 years following the European Protestant Reformation. In his view, which I respect but respectfully reject, the Calvinists didn't make much effort to convert people, and therefore "did little or no mission". Another friend of mine, a pastor in France, used to carry with him a map on which were marked with neat red dots the 600 separate Christian schools that the Calvinists established across France in those same 200 years. Six hundred schools, financed and staffed by passionate followers of Christ and offering a biblically based education to thousands of French children. Is it even remotely fair not to call this mission?

Makoto Fujimura, a Japanese-American artist whose studio is just two blocks from Ground Zero in New York, is both an elder in a Protestant church-plant and a successful and highly regarded expressionist painter. Is he "missional" in the first activity, but not in the second? Is his art, acknowledged by critics as "forging a new kind of art, about hope, healing and redemption, while maintaining visual sophistication and intellectual integrity",[4] not also an expression of his faith? And as he and artists like him wrestle to reflect the beauty of God's kingdom in their work, do they not, as much as the most successful of preaching evangelists, warrant the support and prayers of the church?

The kingdom comes when the will of God is done. The church is truly the church when it works and prays for that to be the case. Mission is everything the people of God do to make the kingdom a present, earth-rooted reality. Church is what we call the process by which we help each other achieve that goal.

Think About It: Last Word on the Last Tango

The death of actress Maria Schneider early in 2011, after a long illness, has revealed the tragic story surrounding one of the most iconic films of the 1970s. *Last Tango in Paris* featured an unknown nineteen-year-old Schneider and the magnetic Marlon Brando in a torrid romance that director Bernardo Bertolucci later admitted was simply the enactment of his own sexual fantasies.

Schneider said that she felt "raped" by the film. She had a breakdown shortly afterwards and never fully recovered, battling for years with drug addiction and moving through serial broken relationships. Brando also claimed that the movie "raped, humiliated and violated" him, and refused for fifteen years to even speak to its director. Both actors said that they wished the film had never been made. And even Bertolucci, speaking after Schneider's death, expressed regret that he had never found occasion to apologize to her. "Maria accused me of having robbed her of her youth," he said, "and only today am I wondering whether there wasn't some truth to that."

What is fascinating about these comments is what they reveal about perspective. In 1972 the film was seen as "sensational". It was received as "art". It pushed the boundaries of cinema for audiences across the world. It broke the mould. It entered the consciousness of millions. But thirty-eight years later *all* the key people involved express regret, and the actors who gave their minds and bodies to the screen use the language of rape.

Culture is not created in a moral vacuum. Art is not beyond the challenge of the kingdom. The stories we tell about ourselves reveal the depths of the narratives we have believed.

The tragedy of Schneider is that, at nineteen, she didn't have a story strong enough to speak a different truth about herself. The tragedy of *The Last Tango* is that a director's grubby fantasy was the best narrative that anyone could come up with. Thirty-eight years later, does this story not cry out for God's prismatic people to shine their light *into, around* and *through* culture?

It is not enough to complain about the films that others make. Where are the films that embody the story God wants to tell about us?

Mission is a Mirror-Ball

*Crucial to the embracing of a "prismatic" understanding
of church is the recognition that the people of God have both a
"gathered" and a "scattered" expression. We are church when we
come together to worship; to learn and grow and build one
another up, but we are also church when we disperse, carrying
God's light into all the different places he takes us.[1]*

Key Text: John 15:5

*Yes, I am the vine; you are the branches. Those who
remain in me, and I in them, will produce much fruit.
For apart from me you can do nothing.[2]*

Abstract

**The mission of God "radiates" out from the church when the
church functions as an equipping community, empowering each
member to shine wherever God takes them.**

While the letters of Paul and Peter are filled with insights into
the New Testament church, the words of Jesus recorded in
the gospels have less to say on the subject. It seems that Jesus
bequeathed to us the community itself and the goals and the
principles it should adhere to, but no blueprint for its structure
or operation.

In the one place Jesus does seem to be describing the church,
though, a powerful picture is given of the kind of community
it will become. John 15 takes a metaphor familiar to Israel, of
God's people as his vineyard or vine, and appropriates it for the
new community the followers of Jesus will form. Eight times

Jesus urges his followers to "abide" in him, and eight times he calls them to "bear fruit".

What is significant in these repeated commands is that they are, in the life of a vine, opposite injunctions. The call to abide is a call to stay close; to cling to the root. It carries, for the church, a sense of "drawing in". But to bear good fruit, a vine moves in the opposite direction. It presses out, away from the root. This is why vine-growers in our day create long, stretched-out fences along which the vines can travel: the best fruit grows when the new shoots are allowed to travel furthest. The call to bear fruit, then, is a call to move out, to get as far from the root as is possible without losing contact.

This carries, for the church, an outward thrust. Thus the one metaphor Jesus does establish for the church introduces the paradox of these two forces: the one drawing us in, to discipleship and intimacy, to closeness and connection; the other thrusting us out, to fruitfulness in the world's far corners. The vine is a unique picture of a plant that thrives by obeying these two distinct commands: staying connected to the root, but pushing out into the field. This is a powerful metaphor for the church.

This same paradox underlies the Pauline vision of church, where the gathering in and sending out of God's people co-exist. Ephesians 4:12 explores the mechanics of how this takes place. How can a gathered, concentrated community be central to God's purposes without becoming the focus of them? How does the light get from the body of the church to the outer edges of our context and culture? The answer lies in what the church does:

> Now these are the gifts Christ gave to the church: the apostles, the prophets, the evangelists, and the pastors and teachers. Their responsibility is to equip God's people to do his work and build up the church, the body of Christ.

This will continue until we all come to such unity in
our faith and knowledge of God's Son that we will be
mature in the Lord, measuring up to the full and complete
standard of Christ.[3]

By equipping each member of the body to fulfil their calling in
Christ, the church "sends out" the light to every corner of the
world. Discipleship and deployment go hand in hand. Personal
growth and purposeful living are two sides of the same coin,
as human beings called to the light of Christ become, more and
more, the carriers of that light. The light of God breaks into
its many constituent colours in the many different callings of
God's people.

In our community in Amsterdam[4] we decided to use not
a prism but a mirror-ball to illustrate this. Sometimes when we
prayed in our auditorium for the fulfilment of God's purposes
in and through our community, we would drop the house lights
and shine a spotlight or two on our mirror-ball, suspended
above the worship space. As we prayed, little squares of light
would begin to move around the room, finding their way into
every corner, poking every dark nook and shadowed cranny.
The central mirror-ball is organized and crafted. It has structure
and intentionality, and a small motor powering its rotation. The
little squares of light are dispersed and creative. They find their
way to different places. The reflecting-out is their equipping.
Focused beams of pure white light break into a shower of tiny
torches when they are sent out in bouncing fragments. It is not a
perfect metaphor, and it was certainly not one available to Paul,
but the mirror-ball is, I believe, a fair image, in physical form, of
the church that Paul is describing.

A prismatic faith is both gathered and dispersed. It has an
expression in which resources are drawn in and concentrated,
when worship and giving and energy and volunteering all
move in an inward direction, to build up and strengthen this

new community. But there is also a dispersed expression, an expression in which every ounce of our energy moves outwards and we seek to resource God's people in every place to which the winds of God will carry them.

The link between the two lies in equipping: an unambiguous, unflinching commitment to find and fulfil the callings of each of God's people. The church becomes a force of transformation and reformation in the culture because the people of God, themselves transformed and reformed through encounter with Christ, become carriers of a different seed; lights projecting a new colour.

In the gathered expression of church we are transformed.

In its dispersed expression we transform.

Drawn in, we are changed. Sent out, we change. Paul's model avoids the creation of a self-centred and self-indulgent community because everything about the gathering is to do with the dispersal. The leadership gifts given to the church are given not to do God's work in the world but to equip those who do. The resulting vision of God's project for his world is summed up in the definition of prismatic church with which this section of the book opened: "all the colours of God's wisdom through all the callings of God's people to every corner of God's world".

Paul's vision of the church radiates colour, like André Derain's painting of Notre Dame des Anges. The *ekklesia*, the assembly of those called out to be followers of Christ, is the vital prism through which God's pure wisdom breaks into its constituent colours. Truth is mediated through human community. God's love takes on shape and colour as it finds expression in reconciled human relationships. There is diversity; variety; originality; idiosyncrasy; the nature of God reflected in a million different hues: the community of grace bursting with colour. Light and colour are restored to God's world. As the Dutch scholar and politician Abraham Kuyper said, "Verily, Christ has swept away the dust with which man's sinful limitations had covered up this world-order, and has made it glitter again in its original brilliancy."[5]

Task #1: Illumination

The language of light used here implies a core task for the people of God. Before we do anything, before we engage in programmes and projects and church-wide campaigns, our simple task is to let God's light shine through us. This is as much about who we are as about what we do. It is as much to do with the places we go every day as the places we go "on mission". It is about our ordinary, everyday lives being infused with the light of God. Everywhere you go God's light can shine as you go. Every person you encounter can be caught in the wonder of that light. Every task you undertake can be illuminated by God's presence.

In the long term there may be specific things God calls you to do. There may be tasks and duties and responsibilities you take on. But in the first instance, this is not what God asks of you. In the first instance, it is what you are already doing that counts. Where you are already going. Who you already know. In these places, among these people, doing these things, let God's light shine through.

Human Church

The Creator has always looked for people who through intimacy and obedience will reflect his character, to bring out "the God-flavors" and "the God-colors" of the world.[1] The New Testament speaks of what God wants to do in people, but also of what he longs to do through people. God's plan has always been to shine through people and since the life, death, resurrection and ascension of Jesus the movement that makes God's shining possible is called "church".[2]

Key Text: 1 Peter 1:12

And now this Good News has been announced to you by those who preached in the power of the Holy Spirit sent from heaven. It is all so wonderful that even the angels are eagerly watching these things happen.[3]

Abstract

The prismatic nature of God's plan shows his determination to shine through people. God's project is a human project. Every human life has potential to shine his light. Human beings are his works of art. Redeemed human beings are pictures at an exhibition.

There is a still deeper truth hidden in Paul's description of the church's prismatic calling. It is a statement that stands in radical continuity with the Hebrew worldview in which Paul was raised: a fulfilment of a promise as old as time itself.

It is buried in a question that I have never heard asked in public: Just what is it about God that the rulers and authorities in the heavenly realms can't already see? It is not clear whether

Paul is talking of angelic or demonic forces, but we are left in no doubt as to where these beings are situated. They dwell in the realm of God. They are not earth-bound but heavenly beings, set in such a context as to be able to look upon God himself. In Paul's Hebrew cosmology there is an earthly, visible realm and there is an invisible, heavenly realm, in which these "rulers and authorities" coexist with God. To borrow imagery from the prologue to the book of Job, these are beings assembled in the Courts of God: whatever their dialogue and interaction with God consists of, it is conducted face-to-face.[4] The God who is invisible to us to them is fully visible, resplendent in all his glory and magnificence. Whatever and whoever else they see, there can be no question that they see God. But there are things about God, Paul asserts, that these beings cannot see; and these things God is determined to show them. To do so he asks the heavenly beings not to look at him, but to look at us.

Imagine you have been set the project of learning about the greatest artists in history. Perhaps Caravaggio or Rembrandt. Perhaps Van Gogh or Picasso. You want to come to a deeper understanding of these great painters; to grasp their genius and their contribution to history. How will you do it? By finding portraits of them and studying their features? You might perhaps learn something, but it will not be much. By reading words they have written, and words written about them? A better option – from this you may well learn important facts.

But a still better option exists, an approach that will open up for you, in time, the very heart of each great artist. You can study their work. In the paintings you will find their genius; the very meaning of their lives. To understand artists, you study their art. And those to whom God wishes to display his wisdom are offered a simple and timeless invitation: "Look at my human creatures." It is in his work, not in himself, that God's greatest glory is seen. The church, the community of redeemed humans who have chosen to journey together as disciples of the risen Christ, is God's most triumphant work of art: redeemed humanity is his *magnum opus*.

There is a clue here, then, not only to what God is doing through the church, but to what God has always been doing. In creation, in Israel, in Jesus and now in the community of his followers, God is fulfilling his election of humanity to shine as his image-bearers in the world. Paul does not see the church as a "new vision" of God's work in the world, as if this task of radiating wisdom has just been invented. Rather, he sees the church as the fulfilment of the oldest vision of all. Ephesians 3:10 is a mirror of Genesis 1:28. God is choosing once again, as he has chosen from the start, to mediate his wisdom through human lives. The mission of God is a prismatic mission because it is utterly – one might almost say obsessively – focused on this goal: to see God's wisdom refracted through the agency of human lives. If luminescence is the property of objects and substances that emit light, God's desire is for his wisdom to be humanescent – shining through human beings.

The radical nature of this statement, buried as it is at the heart of Paul's most compelling account of the calling of the church, is significant for two reasons.

Firstly, because it sets the church firmly in its place in the continuity of salvation history. That which God began in Eden; that which was pictured, in part, in the choosing of Israel; that which is made possible in the human life of Christ – God will now bring to fulfilment through the church. His wisdom will be displayed, and it will be displayed through human agency. Plan A is back on track. The church is the answer to a question asked so long ago that all but God have forgotten it; a question whispered in the moment following the human fall from goodness: "What now?" For millennia God has worked and waited. Through countless generations he has planned and prepared; laying foundations; building expectations; creating the canvas on which his finest work will appear. And now, at last, the miracle can be released: humanity restored, one redeemed life at a time, to its first and true calling at the heart of the created order. Paul's theology of the church and of mission are both rooted in his theology of creation. There is a thread of continuity between that which God has made and that which, in Christ, he is re-making. In the timeless phrase of Al Wolters, the message of the gospel is Creation Regained.[5] And the heart of this miracle is human.

Secondly, it is through people that God's wisdom will shine. If luminescence is the shining of light, then God's plan is humanescent. It is a plan to shine through people. This matters because it calls the church to be as obsessively and passionately concerned with the beauty of human lives as God is. It matters because it holds out a vision of what it is that God wants to do with each human life: to make it shine. Brilliance, nothing less, is God's goal for you, and for each of us. The dullest and most disfigured of human lives are included in God's plans for brilliance. No life is so lost that God's light cannot shine through it. No human is so depraved that God does not desire to pour out his wisdom.

The roots of the kingdom are in God's divinity. It is because God is God that the kingdom is even possible. Without the reality of the God who is wholly other than us, all we've got is us. And "us" has not been good news for planet earth so far. The Godness of God is our hope. But the fruits of the kingdom – the aims and the goals and the projects and the possibilities – are not in God's divinity but in our humanity. The coming of the kingdom doesn't change God – it changes us. Everything about what God wants to do is about what God wants to do in and through us. The kingdom of God is a human kingdom in the sense that a tree that grows apples is an apple tree and a studio that makes films is a film studio. We are the product; the fruit; the result; the work in progress. When God declares a *vernissage* – a preview – for his kingdom exhibition, we are on display: in all the battered beauty of redeemed humanity. Forging love and justice from the raw materials of frail humanity is what God does. God is humanic – obsessively in love with people.

We've been told for years that God is mad with us. It's about time we understood that God is mad about us.

Think About It: The beauty of God

One of the gifts an aesthetic generation is bringing to the church is a renewed appreciation for art, the arts and artfulness. The recovery of art, long overdue in churches obsessed with precisions of truth, has been liberating for many.

But all too often our reflections on art are filed in the category of "creativity". Artists are seen as "creative" people and their gifts are appreciated only so far as they help us to be "creative" in our faith – or in our marketing.

This is valid up to a point, but doesn't go far enough. The category within which art can most revolutionize our lives is not "creativity" but "beauty". Beauty is a category fundamental to the created world, and the search for it obsesses millions. We chase it; fake it; pay for it; idolize it. We falsely tie it to sexuality. We sell short our longing for true beauty and find satisfaction in lesser gods.

Artists, when true to their calling, alert us to beauty. They make signposts to the deeper beauties inherent in the world around us. Their work doesn't need to be married to marketing, or for that matter evangelism, to be justified. To declare beauty is enough. Artists who are also people of faith serve their community by exploring the intimate connection between the beauty of creation and the beauty of the Creator.

To declare God beautiful is mission. Artists are heralds of the beauty of God. Along with recovering the practice of art, the church needs to rediscover a theology of beauty. When was the last time you talked about – or for that matter thought about – the beauty of God?

Fresh from the Factory

*Our primary or fundamental vocation is discipleship – we are called
to follow Christ. But out of this will flow, for each of us, more specific
callings: particular ways in which, in particular places and contexts,
we can obey God, express his character and wisdom and so bring him
glory.*[1]

Key Text: Genesis 1:27–28

*So God created human beings in his own image. In the image of God he
created them; male and female he created them. Then God blessed them
and said, "Be fruitful and multiply. Fill the earth and govern it. Reign
over the fish in the sea, the birds in the sky, and all the animals that
scurry along the ground."*[2]

Abstract

**God's brilliant plan offers us a life of purpose: a life shining
with the dreams of God. Salvation looks beyond rescue and
reconciliation to restoration: human lives shimmering with the
possibilities God has for them. The invitation to follow Christ is
an invitation to embrace our full humanity.**

The assertion that God is determined to shine through people
reframes our understanding of his mission.

God's purpose is not merely to "save" people, redirecting
them from one eternal destination to another: it is to shine,
in all his radiant wisdom, through their lives. Like a collector
and restorer of classic cars, God's work is not done when he
buys a new model. At the point of purchase his work has just
begun. It's not the buying of the car that gives him pleasure,
but the restoration. And until that front wing shines with a

finish as fresh as the day it first left the factory, God will not stop polishing.

With each life restored the aim, Paul states, is "to do good works, which God prepared in advance for us to do".[3] Elsewhere Paul asserts that God's choosing of us took place "before the creation of the world"[4] and that the wisdom he has brought us into is a wisdom "that has been hidden and that God destined for our glory before time began".[5]

The implication is clear: God has plans for each and every life. We are redeemed not into joy alone, but into purpose. Every life has a colour to bring to the party; a light to shine. The mission of God is that I should discover why I was created and live out that purpose to the full.

And God's mission is the same for my neighbour. Even in one life this is a vast project; God's plans for me make Michelangelo's vision for the Sistine Chapel look like doodling. Add to that my neighbour, and my neighbour's neighbour and my neighbour's neighbour's neighbour and you begin to get a sense of the scope of God's mission in the world. Every human life redeemed; alive with purpose; radiant with beauty; fulfilling its potential and bringing its colour to the world – living out the dream God dreamed before his light had even dawned on the world's first day.

This is huge, and at the centre of its hugeness is the church, the seedbed of this new redeemed community. If we are going to engage more fully with God's prismatic purposes, we are going to need a bigger picture of what mission means than that with which our churches have been working.

The Catholic theologian Hans Küng describes this as "The essential difference and superiority of the Christian message, when compared to other oriental religions of redemption." The aim of the Christian faith, he suggests, "is not the salvation of the individual alone and the freeing of the individual soul from suffering, sin and death. The essential part of the Christian message is the idea of salvation for the whole community of people, of which the individual is a member."[6]

Along the road of salvation, I may discover the inestimable joy of being included. I may rejoice to name myself as "saved". But this does not begin to capture the depth and the breadth of God's plan. To take my place in God's plan is to become a part of something bigger and richer and deeper and wider than I can even hope to understand. Citroën cars in France were advertised for many years using the slogan *"Vous n'imaginez pas tout ce que Citroën peut faire pour vous"* – "You can't imagine all that Citroën can do for you." The phrase resonates, for me, with the gospel of the kingdom. This is God's announcement to every human being – helpless and hopeless though they may be: *"Vous n'imaginez pas tout ce que Dieu peut faire avec votre vie."*[7]

The message of the New Testament is an invitation not only to forgiveness and reconciliation, but to purpose and meaning; to usefulness; to beauty. It is an offer of restoration: an invitation to become a human being who shines like the first day out of the factory.

This focus allows us to respond to a question asked of us each day on a thousand billboards and a million television screens: what does it mean to be human? The irony of recent Western history is that the culture that turned its back on God in the name of humanism seems to have, as a result, less knowledge than ever of what being human means. Our society defines us by what we earn; by what we own; perhaps at times by what we produce. In its weakest moments it defines us by what we consume.

God's story, by contrast, defines us by what we are called to be. Standing apart from us, addressing us from a position of objectivity, our Creator speaks purpose to our lives by giving us a task.

We are asked to care for the created world; to develop its potential and fulfil its possibilities. We are asked to do this not by our own wit alone but with the wisdom of God, as his image-bearers in the world. This "calling" or "mandate" is described in Scripture in the language of election: from among the creatures and from among the animals in particular, only the man and the woman are chosen for this task. Humans are elected, set apart, as the creatures through whom the Creator's wisdom will be mediated. Adam's first act as steward of God's garden – the naming of his fellow animals – clearly sets out his place and purpose. We are one with the created order, unquestionably part of it and identified in our very DNA as animal, and yet we are set apart from it, given the gifts and capacities needed to care for and "rule over" our fellow creatures.

But you don't need Scripture to tell you that this is true: the evidence is all around you. The evidence is you. Language; community; the use of tools – all these are signs of the spark that God has given us.

Proof of this is not hard to find. Take, for example, the British chef Jamie Oliver. All animals eat, and most enjoy their food. There is nothing in the capturing and consuming of food that is especially human. But only humans cook, and only humans talk about their cooking. There is no Jamie Oliver for the lions; no Gordon Ramsay for the apes. The very existence of such cooks is proof of the expectations God has of humanity. We are uniquely gifted, capable of shaping and directing the created world and speaking innovation into being, and with our gifting comes unique responsibility. It is to this responsibility that Jesus is referring when he calls all who will listen to rediscover their God-given role in the world:

> *You are the salt of the earth. But what good is salt if it has lost its flavour? Can you make it salty again? It will be thrown out and trampled underfoot as worthless.*
> *You are the light of the world—like a city on a hilltop that cannot be hidden. No one lights a lamp and then puts*

it under a basket. Instead, a lamp is placed on a stand, where it gives light to everyone in the house. In the same way, let your good deeds shine out for all to see, so that everyone will praise your heavenly Father.[8]

It is Israel that Jesus is critiquing here, and the church that he is anticipating, but ultimately it is to humans, as humans, that this appeal is addressed.

The biblical narrative offers a high and holy calling to humanity. How tragic that so many have looked to humanism because they did not find, in the church, a deep enough or rich enough conception of the calling of humanity. Can we recover, in our embracing of the mission of God in our world, a full-colour vision of human life redeemed? Can we take our place around the human table, ready to contribute a God-soaked perspective to the issues there discussed?

To get to such a vision from where we are now, huddled in our squat grey buildings watching the populations of Europe leave, is quite a journey. It will require the recovery of forgotten wavelengths in the story of God. It will call us to a wider understanding of God's mission in the world, to a deeper engagement with human culture and to a stronger than ever commitment to the equipping of God's people. But it will offer us, in return, the colours of God.

Think About It: What shall we grow here?

The poem "What Shall We Grow?" is about marriage. It was written for the wedding of my son Aaron to Holly in May 2011. But like the picture Genesis gives of Adam and Eve in Eden, it is about much more than marriage. It is about what we do as humans in the garden God has given us. And in a sense it is about the church. What will we do, together, with the wonders God has given us?

What Shall We Grow?

What shall we grow
    In this garden God has given us?
        What seeds shall we sow in this safe circle?
            What fruits can we have faith for?
                What wonders might we work?
                    In this polychrome parade
                    Of newfound names
                    That claims and frames us?
If we merge
    Our minds and muscles
        What marvels might we make?
            What miracles can our creator craft
                From our surrendered strengths?
In this walled place
    Of waterfalls
        And wells in the wilderness
        This green gathering
            Of growth and goodness
        This cathedral
            of branches and light
                Describing,
                    Designing,
                        Defining sacred space
            This folded fabric of trailing vines
                This joy of undiscovered pathways
                    This innocent exuberance of safety
Our secret sabbath
    Our hidden home
        Our Eden
            What shall we grow here?
            We shall grow old together
            What shall we sow here?
            We shall sow love [9]

Your Call is Important to Us

There is no limit to the "where" of God's desire to shine through his people: every corner of the world is included.[1]

Key Text: Ephesians 2:10

For we are God's masterpiece. He has created us anew in Christ Jesus, so we can do the good things he planned for us long ago.[2]

Abstract

The breadth of God's kingdom project calls for a broader understanding of mission, and for a broader recognition of the callings of God's people. Vocation is not for the elite few but for all. All are called, just as all are gifted, and there is no limit to the vision God may have for every human life.

Mission is about the contest between God and idols; about whether our lives will honour and proclaim the wonders of a piece of carved stone, or sing out the glories of our living Creator. Where I wrestle to suppress the former and magnify the latter, and where I help others to do the same, I am engaging in God's mission in the world.

So acts of compassion are missional when they let love shine where hate might otherwise reign. When acts of compassion are conditional on a certain cerebral response, or offered as bribes toward changes in belief and behaviour, they are not in essence missional.

Forgiveness is missional where it lets grace flow where bitterness has been. Where forgiveness comes wrapped in

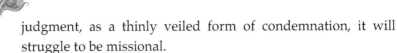

judgment, as a thinly veiled form of condemnation, it will struggle to be missional.

Art is missional when through love of God and neighbour it honours the beauty of the Creator. When art distorts the image of God in the world, or hides his light, it is anything but missional. Even if the figure in the picture is Jesus.

Evangelism is missional when it helps people to discover that they are made by a loving Creator – fashioned on purpose and for a purpose. When evangelism harangues people with words they cannot understand about the anger of a God they cannot love, it is anything but missional. Even if the meetings are in a church.

Banking is missional when it wrestles with the love of mammon, and seeks not so much to profit from the rich as to bless and help the poor.

Picking up litter is missional when it is motivated by love of God and neighbour.

Central to the outworking of this vision is the recovery of the concept of vocation. The word comes from the Latin for "to call", and has intimations of a spoken or vocal calling. It refers to the God-given callings we choose to follow. Vocation has been misused over the years in two key ways. In the first, it is applied only to paid employment – referring always to the job you do. So "baker", "banker" and "babysitter" are all vocations. In the second it refers more specifically to the call of God, but only applies to those committed to "full-time" service of the church. This is the sense in which the word is used today in Catholic circles, where "vocations" are limited to priests, monks and nuns. The "crisis in vocations" refers to the decline in the numbers of people offering themselves to such a life.

Both of these uses have merit, and rightly display aspects of what vocation means, but neither does it full justice. To give the word its fuller meaning, vocation refers to anything you do in response to the call of God. It is a course of action you follow or an act of service you offer because you have sensed the call of God to do so. The life of the church is prismatic because of the great variety and spread of the callings received by God's people. The light of the mirror-ball bounces out widely into the culture because there are so many different spheres and activities to which God's people are called. The role of the church, at the heart of God's mission, is to help all God's people to discover their vocations. What is God calling you to do?

To think vocationally is to seek the call of God to the particular sphere of society or area of culture on which my life has most impact, and to serve God's purposes in that setting. For some this is the workplace – though not for all. There are those for whom paid employment is an income-generating necessity, rather than a calling, and vocation surfaces instead in voluntary activities outside the workplace, or in the love and care offered in the home or to neighbours. There are as many ways of loving God and neighbour as there are shades of colour in the spectrum of white light and a vocation is as unique, and as personal, as a fingerprint. Finding your vocation is discovering what you were made to do. Evelyn and James Whitehead write: "Vocation is a gradual revelation – of me to myself by God... It is who we are, trying to happen."[3]

Perhaps the most graphic biblical model of a vocation recognized and realized is the call of Moses. After forty years of identity confusion and forty more of exile and struggle, Moses meets the God Yahweh in the burning bush and is called to a task that miraculously makes sense of his life and history. A dynamic triangle is established in which Moses' character, gifts and backstory fall into line with the purposes of God in the earth and with the evident and urgent need of the Hebrew people. Moses receives a call that fits him like a glove – to the extent that no other Hebrew is remotely close to being able to fulfil it. The call moves forward the purposes of God in history and addresses the very real suffering of the Hebrew slaves.

To move into this triangle, where my gifts are expressed, God's purposes move forward, and the needs of the oppressed are met, is to move into vocation.

There is much more that could be said of the call of Moses, and more besides of the cast of thousands who together form the "great cloud of witnesses" brought to life in the Bible's pages, but the simple truth is this: Scripture boldly proclaims the possibility of each of us finding and fulfilling our vocational calling. All are gifted, Paul suggests.[4] All are called to works "prepared in advance for us to do".[5] All are moving towards a place of maturity whose only viable measure is the very stature of Christ.[6] And in that word *all*, we see the breadth of God's missional panorama: God's passion is as wide as the human race itself, and as colourful.

It will take a lifetime to truly come to understand where mission begins and ends – perhaps that's what the path of discipleship is about: surrendering more and more of ourselves so that more and more of God shines through. But Paul seems confident that it is possible to make a start, that with the tools God gives us we can indeed discern his mission in the world.

A vocational understanding of our participation in God's mission tells us three things about our discipleship.

Firstly, it tells us that the mark and the measure of God's missional endeavour is the presence of human thriving. Where humans flourish in their gifting, revelling in love and purpose and oozing with love of God and neighbour, the colours of God's goodness are seen. The end of evangelism is not scalps collected: it is human thriving. God calls each of us not to rescue alone, but to purpose – to the discovery, development and deployment of the gifts he has given us. The educationalist Ken Robinson reports a conversation with Paul McCartney, who says that he "went through his entire education without anyone noticing that he had any musical talent at all. He even applied to join the choir of Liverpool Cathedral and was turned down. They said he wasn't a good enough singer."[7]

Is McCartney an exception to the human rule, an unusually talented individual who simply wasn't "spotted" as a child? Or is he an example of the experience of millions, where God-given gifts lie undiscovered and unused because we don't seek our vocation, or encourage others into theirs? Can the church become the one place on earth where all are empowered to find out who they are and why God made them?

Secondly, this tells us that everyone counts. Paul's letter to the Ephesians is shot through with "alls", and it is from all of us that he longs to see light shine. A recent UK-based ad campaign for the Royal Marine Corps carried the strapline "99.9% need not apply".[8] The ads showed how tough Marine training is; how only the strongest survive; how you won't get through without grit and determination and an almost supernatural strength. The implication is clear: only a very few are fit enough for this. Only a few of the few will make it. The rest of you needn't bother even filling in the form.

Such an appeal couldn't be further from the view of the gospel presented in Ephesians. Here all are gifted. All have potential. All can be redeemed. All have purpose. And the work won't be done until all have reached to the very measure of the stature of Christ.[9] This is a sweeping, comprehensive view of the potential of humanity from which no one is excluded. 100 per cent can apply. 100 per cent will be received. And the job won't be considered done until 100 per cent have discovered their vocations and are thriving in them.

Thirdly, this tells us what to do with our prayers. We do not pray for the addict on the corner of our street to be merely "saved" from addiction. We pray for her to thrive; to find life; to give and receive love; to prosper in her giftings and make a wondrous contribution to her world. We do not pray for "decisions for Christ" – we pray for works of art. And if we can't imagine such works of art, if we can't believe people capable of such beauty, then we will not find ourselves able to pray. "If God can do more than we can ask or imagine,"[10] the missiologist Dan Davidson writes, "why not ask for more imagination?"[11] Prayer is the act of imagining how things can be in the redemptive purposes of God and determining to hold to that imagination even in the face of how things are. And this includes what people – all people – can, by God's grace, become.

Have we lost our vision for the church because we have lost our vision of what people can be? Are we infused with the same overwhelming, unstoppable commitment to the potential of people that carried the eternal Christ to a stable, a cross and a throne?

Think About It: Holy grounding

What must it have meant to Moses to be told that he stood on holy ground? He was, in effect, grounded. A wanted murderer in Egypt; a profound embarrassment to his adopted royal family; living in a country he didn't want to live in; doing a job he didn't want to do, Moses had no way out.

And all the time he fumed that the Hebrew slaves didn't, either. His efforts to help his people had failed. He was racked with guilt, overwhelmed by the sense of his own powerlessness. Apart from the relative compensation of an apparently good marriage and a supportive father-in-law, on most other indicators Moses is, by the time he sees the burning bush, down and out. And then he hears God's voice, and God declares the ground on which he stands holy: the very ground of his grounding.

Whatever happened in Moses' head and heart at that moment, it gave him courage to face a challenge he had been running from for forty years. Like the alcoholic who at last signs in to AA; the prodigal who turns towards home; the unsigned song-writer who finally presses "record", Moses turns to face his fears and breaks the deadlock of his grounding. What makes the difference? The discovery that God is with him in his exile. God is never "over there" but always "right here". Moses' holy ground is not some distant dream it will take years, and miles, to reach. It is here. It is now.

Quietly, consistently, under the surface of exile, God has been preparing one of the greatest religious and political leaders in the history of humanity, whose bold imagination will in time not only free the Hebrew slaves but set a template for human societies across the world for generations to come. Through forty years of struggle God has been sowing into Moses the gifts and experiences he will need for the journey ahead. With the burning bush encounter that preparation breaks the surface, and Moses comes to see that God is with him, has always been with him and will be with him in all the adventures to come. Old; tired; guilty; flawed; washed-up; burnt-out; spent – Moses becomes the beginning of a global revolution.

In a dead-end job? Overwhelmed with failure? Convinced you'll never amount to anything? The shortest distance in the known universe is the distance between where you are right now and where you need to be to hear God's voice and move on. Whatever God might want to achieve through you; whatever revolutions are about to start; whatever he has been preparing you for – it begins with meeting him right now, holy on the very ground of your grounding.

Task #2: Vocation

To understand that God calls each person to influence some part of his world is to accept a strong and powerful calling for the church. We are to be a vocational community – a body of people who help each other to find the place God wants them to be and the things God wants them to do. Moses had a burning bush, but we have each other. Can we see in one another the potential of God's shining? Is there a shepherd in your church in whom you see the calling of a Moses?

What kind of community do we need to be to encourage one another in vocation? How can we help each other to find our gifts; to hear God's voice; to move in the things the Holy Spirit has for us? If the choreographer Gillian Lynne had come to your church as a child, would you have seen the dancer in her?

God's Brilliant Idea #2:
"Give Them Power!"

The church as a charismystic community

charismatic (ˌkarizˈmatik)

Adjective: exercising a compelling charm that inspires devotion in others; of or relating to the charismatic movement in the Christian church; (of a power or talent) divinely conferred.
Noun: an adherent of the charismatic movement; a person who claims divine inspiration.

mystic (ˈmistik)

Noun: a person who seeks by contemplation and self-surrender to obtain unity with or absorption into the Deity or the absolute, or who believes in the spiritual apprehension of truths that are beyond the intellect.
Adjective: another term for **mystical:** of or relating to mystics or religious mysticism; spiritually allegorical or symbolic; transcending human understanding; inspiring a sense of spiritual mystery, awe, and fascination.

charismystic (ˌkarizˈmistik)

Adjective: in awe of heaven, rooted in earth.

Charismystic Community

Every cloud
has a sacred lining.
The sparkle of the spirit
nestles in the everyday.
Give me eyes to see God,
and a heart and words to praise.[1]

Key Text: Ephesians 4:4

For there is one body and one Spirit, just as you
have been called to one glorious hope for the future.[2]

Abstract

In the coming-together of monastic and charismatic spiritualities, ancient and modern expressions of faith, God is reminding us of the place of spiritual formation in the church. The Holy Spirit is forming us to be like Christ. The call to mission is a call to spiritual formation.

Sagres, on the extreme south-western coast of Portugal, used to be the end of the world. Its cliff-top fortress housed an ancient school of navigation and overlooked an ocean that, as far as sailors were concerned, was dangerous and uncrossable: the beginning of the end of everything. An unrecognized reef not far offshore, churning and foaming with the incoming tide, even led to the belief that the sea was boiling: clear confirmation that nothing lay beyond. By the fifteenth century every other ocean in the world had been crossed, but the Atlantic remained a mystery. The final frontier. A pit of terrors at the very edge of a flat and finite earth.

Across the bay from Sagres, visible from the ramparts of the fort, the lighthouse of Cape Saint Vincent stands guard over the most south-westerly point on the European continent. Steep, high cliffs drop suddenly to a hostile sea, and the winds on this exposed cape blow with constant fury.

Part-way between the fort and the lighthouse lie the ruins of another ancient building – a Franciscan monastery clinging to the cliff face. Sir Francis Drake included the monastery in his campaign to establish British supremacy wherever a landing from sea made it possible. He attacked and burnt it in 1587. Now partially restored, high stone walls surround a small chapel and chapter house. Thick iron posts mark the path of a rugged stairway cut into the side of the cliff, giving the monks access to the sea and, no doubt, exclusive fishing rights.

The monastery is essentially uninhabited, though preserved as a national monument. The fort has become an attractive museum with a shop and café for the tourists. The lighthouse remains functional, though without the once necessary residential team. The co-location of these three distinct buildings on this windswept peninsula is a powerful symbol of the blended histories of Europe – the lighthouse ensuring the safety and prosperity of trade and commerce; the fort offering defence and training for war; the monastery between the two ensuring that here, at the wildest edge of Europe, there should be a place of prayer.

It was on this wild and rough-hewn coast, in the closing years of the twentieth century, that a new prayer movement was born that would come to influence a generation across the planet. Pete Greig, at the time the leader of a youth church on the south coast of England, came here to pray. Something about the wildness of the landscape, the rugged history of empires and explorers, merchants and monks, and the more recent influx of young people drawn to some of the best surf beaches in Europe, caught his imagination. As he prayed he looked northeastwards, back across the European continent, and saw, as in a vision, a new army of young people, owning an ancient faith and rising in a post-modern world to pray. To this visionary young leader the experience served as a sign that something remarkable, something new was happening among the young people of Europe. The potency of the long-held Christian creeds was not dead, as so many had assumed: there was power yet to inspire a new generation.

The vision he had at Cape Saint Vincent started Pete Greig on a journey that culminated in the formation of the 24-7 prayer movement, a dynamic movement of young people that has since touched every continent and continues to inspire creative, passionate prayer and mission.[3] The movement has grown into a global, uninterrupted prayer-meeting that in 2010 celebrated its first decade of life.

Perhaps surprisingly, in view of Pete Greig's own background in the very contemporary, very Protestant "new churches" of the United Kingdom, the 24-7 prayer movement has also become one of the focal points of a recovery, across Western culture, of monastic spirituality, widely referred to as "the New Monasticism". Touched by stories of the Desert Fathers and Celtic saints and the writings of Benedict, Francis, Theresa and many others, young people at the experimental edge of Pentecostal and charismatic experience are re-engaging with the ancient spiritualities that fed the prayer life of Europe for unnumbered generations. One of Greig's most recent books, *Punk Monk*[4] – written with "Abbot" Andy Freeman – captures the strangeness of this unexpected convergence, with the most nonconformist and iconoclastic of young people, tattoos and dreadlocks to the fore, seeking structure and rhythm in "rule-of-life" spirituality. The parish of St Thomas Crookes in Sheffield has formed "TOM" – The Order of Mission – to experiment with a rule of life adapted to young, urban professionals, many of whom have reduced their paid employment to part-time hours in order to free up time for community and vocational service. The emphasis is on sustainable spirituality, blending the ancient commitments and rhythms of monastic prayer with the demands of the contemporary city.

In Germany, Mark and Nadine Reichman[5] were among the young leaders most influenced by and active in the 24-7 movement in their own nation. Together they planted and led a "post-modern church" in Karlsruhe, with an Arts Café, diverse community projects and an approach to worship that appealed to the city's large alternative community.

But after ten years of constant action and activity, they stepped away from this life, exhausted and not a little confused. They longed for an approach to life and mission that was more sustainable, less grounded in a high-energy rush from one frantic project to the next. They longed for rhythm; for Sabbath; for a faith that flowed out from a place of rest. The result of their quest is "Bethanien",[6] a new and hip community founded in a convent borrowed from the Catholic "Schonstatt" movement. The community is home to a creative collective called "Mateno",[7] publishers of the *über*-artful *Froh* magazine.[8] With its tiny chapel set among the trees and its monastic arrangement of bedrooms and communal spaces, Bethanien hardly seems the place for a future-focused faith community to be founded. But that is what is happening as young Germans come together to seek a deeper, more authentic walk of faith: a remarkable collision of post-modern aspirations and ancient faith-practices.

Across the Atlantic the church-planter Karen Ward, an internet-savvy, streetwise community activist, has formed an "urban abbey" within the Episcopal church and is both Abbess and Vicar.[9] With a significant blog and Twitter presence, the Church of the Apostles brings the spiritual disciplines of pre-Reformation Europe to the web-cafés of post-modern Seattle. Fellow "emergent Anglican" Ian Mobsby, one of the leaders of London's "Moot" community, has also written extensively on the post-modern potential of ancient monastic practices. The "rhythm" of the Moot community is a leading example of a rule of life shaped for a contemporary urban setting.[10]

What these disparate movements have in common is a desire to blend the strength of ancient, proven disciplines with the flexibility of a post-modern faith, and in many cases with the immediacy of charismatic experience. The ground that, for centuries, Christian mystics have explored – the meeting-point of spirit and flesh, where the waves of a supernatural ocean crash on nature's shores – is once again the seedbed of mission. This is a charismystic generation; explorers of the wild roads of spirituality; committed to adventuring with God; seeking a journey as deep in the disciplines as it is strong in the Spirit.

Converging from the other side of the Reformational divide, the Franciscan Friars of the Renewal are a new monastic movement founded in the late 1980s in the Bronx, New York. In 2007, they established their newest friary in Ireland's most notorious neighbourhood – Limerick's Moyross estate. Robed and shaven-headed, the bearded brothers have won the hearts of the local population, plagued as they are by vandalism, drug crime and joy-riding. The journalist Rory Fitzpatrick describes succinctly the appeal of these unexpected local heroes: "In an age of celebrity, they practise humility; in an age where everything is sexualised, they vow chastity; in an age of consumerism, they vow poverty. They walk through the world showing us there is another way."[11] Like most European nations, Ireland has seen the congregations and the credibility of its churches implode in recent years. The Catholic Church is rocked to its core by scandal. Recruiting new priests has become all but impossible. In this crisis situation the Friars, Fitzpatrick writes, "provide hope that, against the odds, a better church might emerge".[12]

The shift towards a more monastic faith is more than a fad in church life. It is indicative of a deeper change; a mood-shift in the culture in which post-modern seekers, disdainful of modernity's brash certainties, look for the deeper truths buried in pre-modernity. Plundering the past, they fund their future. The church that wins the hearts of this generation will not be programme-driven or meeting-dependent, nor will it be a one-day-a-week experience. It will be life-wide, exploring the spiritual implications of the ordinary; finding energy in the everyday. It will have rhythm and community; shared meals and sustainable practices. It will bear the marks of the old and the new; of ancient creeds poured into new-made moulds. Above all, it will be a spiritual community: a church founded on the shared call to explore the spiritual life.

Western culture is witnessing a movement of "convergence" in which charismatic, contemplative, sacramental and social-justice spiritualities are being woven together and a picture of an ancient–future church is emerging. Beyond the boundaries of the intentional and identifiable new communities that make up the new monasticism, there are perhaps tens of thousands of individual Christians, members for the most part of mainstream churches, who are finding new energy and inspiration from their engagement with these ancient practices. Where modernity devalued the past in favour of present experience, post-modernity seeks inspiration in the ancient, shopping in the past to fund the future.

Diverse as these expressions of a "new monasticism" are, they flow from a shared belief that the ancient wisdom of the European monastic traditions may yet have resources to offer in post-modern times. Many of the young adults drawn to these new communities are, like the founders of the 24-7 prayer movement, drawn from the Pentecostal and charismatic churches of the twentieth century. Usually traced back to events at a small chapel on Azusa Street in Los Angeles in 1906, the Pentecostal and charismatic movements have reshaped the global church in just over 100 years. They represent the most recent developments in church history and boast some of the fastest growing and, in style, most contemporary churches.

But a new generation is already questioning some of the assumptions common to many of these churches, in particular their valuing of experience over tradition and their focus on the present acts of God at the expense of continuity and solidarity with God's actions in history. Young charismatics are seeking a blend of new and old, marrying the dynamic energy of Pentecostalism with the ancient resources of history. They do so because of a belief, captured in the words of the Dutch priest Henri Nouwen, that spirituality must somehow touch the everyday. God cannot simply be the main attraction at meetings: he must be the mystery that runs through everything. Nouwen wrote in 1997:

> *The ideal of the monk is to live in the presence of God,*
> *to pray, read, work, eat, and sleep in the company of the*
> *divine Lord. Monastic life is the continuing contemplation*
> *of the mysteries of God, not just during the periods of*
> *silent meditation but during all parts of the day. In so far*
> *as the monastery is the place where the presence of God*
> *in the world is most explicitly manifest and brought to*
> *consciousness, it is indeed the centre of the world.*[13]

This eclectic blending of spiritual sources – the ancient and the post-modern colliding in a shower of sparks – touches on the rediscovery of a thread that is crucial to Christian history, recognizing that charismatic and Pentecostal experiences belong to the mystical dimension of faith. Evelyn Underhill, in the classic 1915 work *Practical Mysticism*, describes mysticism as "the art of union with reality. The mystic is a person who has attained that union in greater or less degree; or who aims at and believes in such attainment." Contemporary explorers of these phenomena stand in a long line and tradition dating back 2,000 years. For the new monastics God's mystery is everywhere, pervading the very atoms of the earth. Where the mystery of God meets the landscapes of our world; where the oceans of heaven lap on the shores of earth; in that mystical place where the here and now is infused, somehow, with the essence of a world beyond: at that borderline there is energy to be experienced and life to be explored.

What the charismystics are discovering is an approach to faith that integrates prayer with mission and permeates the whole of life. They find, in ancient resources, a way to overcome the dualism of modern Christianity and carry a faith commitment into every corner of their lives. This is a spirituality rooted in the creation; alive to the everyday; fuelled in contemplation and fulfilled in action. It is a whole-life journey with, at its heart, a dynamic spiritual quest: to grow in relationship with God and to live meaningfully in God's world. Questions of mission and justice sit alongside questions of worship and spirituality: the desire is for a rhythm of life that connects the inward and the outward worlds and marries prayer with purpose and religion with reality.

A second idea as ancient as that of vocation is growing in its capacity to inspire this adventurous generation. Formation, largely lost to the contemporary church but re-emerging among charismystic seekers, summarizes this process of connecting the inner life with life lived actively and outwardly. If vocation is the process by which my life and work, the way I use my time and offer my gifts, are surrendered to God in obedience and trust for the growth of his kingdom, formation is the process by which this is achieved. It is a traditional way of describing the path of discipleship, and points to a disciplined personal journey towards union with God.

A more deliberate term than discipleship, formation is the process of spiritual growth and discovery. It is deeper than head knowledge but more solid than heart feelings. It is relational and creational, an adventure of learning as a follower of Christ in the world. It is the opening-up of the deepest parts of our selves to God's light and the working-out of God's purposes for every area of our lives. Where the term discipleship is too often used restrictively to describe the early months or years of faith, formation is a lifelong process.

Formation is one of the primary reasons for the church to be established as community. It is a journey that cannot be undertaken alone. Formation thrives in the context of reconciled relationships. And just as vocation is for all, so formation is for all – leaders and followers alike; professional centre-stage Christians and sideline onlookers; old and young; experienced and new-born. Many of the texts inspiring a new generation were written in the first instance for ordained people – priests, nuns and monks seeking a life of special holiness. But if there is to be no dualism in the church, no sacred/secular divide, then formation and vocation must surely extend more widely than priests and pastors. Vocation, as Os Guinness explores in his excellent book *The Call*, is for all God's people.[14] And the young charismystics are discovering this is also true of formation – reading Benedict's *Rule of Life* on their journey to the office or, like the "Moot" community, committing to a shared rhythm created specifically for the urban, working setting. Monastic spirituality is finding new life in the market-place.

This picture of the life of faith as a spiritual adventure, lived at the borderlines of heaven and earth and dependent on the presence of God's Spirit in the created world and in the believer, is remarkably consistent with the New Testament portrait of the church. For Paul, the prismatic calling of the church – the releasing of the people of God into their polychrome vocational callings – is entirely built on the work of the Holy Spirit. Ephesians 4 offers insight into the mechanics of the church, exploring just how the vision of Ephesians 3:10 will be delivered. And it does so by reference to the work of the Holy Spirit in the life of each believer. The church can only be God's prismatic people to the extent that it is also a charismystic community – the very temple in which the Holy Spirit dwells. To engage with God's mission through us, we must of necessity engage with God's mission in us. To go further we must go deeper. A generation believing we are all in some sense monks, called to "pray, read, work, eat, and sleep in the company of the divine Lord", living out in the everyday world a spirituality as vital as that of the Desert Fathers, is remarkably in tune with the vision of Ephesians 4. The call to mission is a call to spiritual formation.

Think About It: More desert, anyone?

Many contemporary Christians resist the concept of spiritual formation because it sounds a lot like hard work. We see discipline as the opposite of freedom, and use the phrase "a desert time" negatively. Dallas Willard, in his 1988 classic *The Spirit of the Disciplines*,[15] suggests that we are wrong to do so. He considers the forty days Jesus spent in the wilderness before confronting temptation and evil and a face-to-face battle with the enemy of his soul. Because we see the desert as negative and fasting as deprivation, Willard says, we think of Jesus as reduced to his greatest place of weakness before this confrontation takes place. But what if the reverse is true? What if the Holy Spirit takes Jesus into the desert to make him stronger for the battle? What if the forty days is a boot-camp, detox and fitness regime rolled into one, bringing Jesus to tip-top, world-beating warrior condition to face his foe? What if the place of silence and retreat, of fasting and discipline and being alone with God – the wilderness of prayer and encounter – is precisely where we need to go to be made strong? How might that change the way we view the disciplines today?

The modern-day Desert Father Charles de Foucault said:

We must cross the desert and spend some time in it
to receive the grace of God as we should. It is there
that one empties oneself, that one drives away from
oneself everything that is not God and that one empties
completely the small house of one's soul so as to leave all
the room for God alone.[16]

The writer Sara Maitland has researched over many years the place of silence and solitude in the contemporary world. Of her experiments with desert living, she says:

In the desert I learned that silence is more for me than a
context for prayer, or a way of creating more time (though
those are important). It is, in itself, a form of freedom; it
generates freedom, free choices, inner clarity, strength. A
freedom from oneself and a freedom to be oneself.[17]

Can the spirituality of the desert, associated not with prosperity and plenty, but with deprivation and discipline, be recovered for a post-modern age? Can we find, in ancient disciplines, new joy?

Task #3: Formation

All too often spiritual formation is seen as a lone calling. Those who pursue most ardently the deeper things of God can find themselves drawn away from, instead of into, local church life. But what if "formation for all" became the very life of the church? What would it take for our projects and programmes to be centred on such a vision of human growth?

To make formation central to the church is to pursue *discipleship* not as a beginner's course in Christianity but as a lifelong journey. It is to see the development of God's people as the key to God's mission. It is to recognize that the bread-

and-butter of the church's call is investment in people. Jesus calls me to love God with "heart, soul, mind and strength" and to love my neighbour unreservedly. My growth in such love is formation. My heart healed. My soul refreshed. My mind renewed. My strength surrendered to God's purposes. It is love taking up residence in me, asserting its presence, extending the inner territory to which it lays claim. How can my engagement with God's people, the church, foster such a journey? Can my membership of the church become, by definition, the fuel of my transformation?

Discovering Fire

Transformation by the power of the Spirit is not a spectacular,
otherworldly process. It is embedded in life's realities;
worked out in the highs and lows of our everyday world.[1]

Key Text: Acts 2:3

Then, what looked like flames or tongues of fire appeared and settled on
each of them. And everyone present was filled with the Holy Spirit...[2]

Abstract

Born in the gift of fire, the adventure of church is fuelled by
the generosity of God. Flames of gifted empowerment hover
over each and every head, as the Creator offers to his creatures
the very presence of his Spirit. Our engagement in our Maker's
mission is dependent on his gifts, and the different gifts
given to each of us all have their place.

Formation, for the Christian, is the pursuit of union with ultimate reality through the path set out by Jesus.

Formation does not see spiritual growth as an escape from reality, but as a discovery of the God whose life is the very pulse of reality. It is faith forged in the real world. It takes full account of what is and seeks to know more of the God who is found in what is. Formation is a collision between two worlds – God's and mine – and seeks to read the landscapes of my life in the language God gives to me.

Philosopher Dallas Willard suggests that six dimensions form the essence of human nature – thought, feeling, choice, body, social context, and soul – and that Christian formation consists in bringing all six under submission to God, resulting in "love of God with all of the heart, soul, mind and strength, and of the neighbor as oneself".[3] "Whatever my action is," Willard writes, "comes out of my whole person." Formation – which he calls "the renovation of the heart" – is the process by which, as a whole person, I come more and more to emulate Christ. It connects my spiritual journey with my journey through the world.

The prismatic church described in Ephesians is a community that touches the world because all of its members experience this formation. The "why" of church is God's light diffused into creation. The "how" is formation and vocation: a billion different colours of light shining through a million different windows.

In Ephesians 4 Paul attributes this formation to the Holy Spirit. This is a Spirit-soaked chapter. The description of the church found there is both mystical and charismatic. Mystical because it is grounded in the fabric of creation, where the breath of God breathes life into his creatures and each one of us is called to respond. Charismatic because the whole operation, from start to finish and at all points in between, is gift-oriented.

Paul has a Jewish pneumatology, understanding that the Spirit touches on every aspect of life. He declares in Athens to the pagan Greeks that God is the one who "gives life and breath to everything"; the one in whom we all "live and move and exist".[4] He knows from the Hebrew Scriptures that the Holy Spirit has been present in creation, brooding over a formless ocean and breathing life into clay-shaped lungs; that the same Holy Spirit leads and liberates the Hebrew slaves, holding back an ocean by his breath alone; visits David in praise and Elijah in proclamation; promises through Ezekiel and Joel a new age of heart intimacy between God and his people. He knows that this same Spirit has hovered over Jesus and worked through him in healing and teaching and the ministry of forgiveness; has raised the lifeless body of the Messiah to triumphant life. And he knows now that this same Spirit falls on and fills the waiting people of God and is active in the life of every believer. He who has been God from the beginning and will be God beyond the end is present now, indwelling and empowering those who seek him. This empowerment, the gift of God to each believer, is the fundamental fuel of mission.

When I was a child and moved with my family to Paris, I faced the mountaineering-like task of learning French. One of the tools that helped me to do so was a book – a beautiful picture-book whose limited number of words on each page were the first I learned to read in my new language. The book was called *The Story of Fire*. It followed a fictionalized account of what it must have been like on the night that a human family, for the first time, made a fire. Once domesticated, fire changed everything. Even in a telling aimed at young children, this story captured something of the enormity of this discovery. On the night the first camp fire burnt, the book told me, the world, and our place in it, changed. So when I read in Acts 2 of the coming of the Spirit, I am moved to discover that this event, too, centres on the gift of fire: tongues of flame resting on the heads of all those who had gathered to pray. I sense two profound connections between this text and my childhood reading of the story of fire.

The first is that this day, too, changed everything. Not just for those present, and not just for the church, but for everyone. Pentecost is a giant leap in the human journey. For Paul it is the moment that makes the church possible; that opens up God's purposes; that reveals at last the secret plan hidden from time immemorial: to shine through people. The gift of fire changes history.

The second connection is, for me, deeper still. It is that the same Holy Spirit is at work in both events. The Spirit of Pentecost is the Spirit of creation, who has lovingly watched over the human journey from the very start. However and whenever it was that the first human harnessing of fire took place, it took place by the generous inspiration of God's Spirit. The spark that makes us human, that sets us apart from our fellow animals, is God's gift to us. Language and tool-making, so central to the Pentecost event – where tongues are loosed and gifts are given – are the two most foundational ingredients of the human difference. Even with evidence of primitive language systems and the use of tools in primates, the human difference remains stark. He who made us, who has given us the tasks and roles of human thriving, comes to us in a new gift of fire that will empower our journey further still. The Spirit comes at Pentecost not to break us free or distract us from our human calling, but to empower us in it.

There is rich continuity, then, in the way Paul presents the present work of the Holy Spirit. He is the gift-giver, the one who brings to the gifts given to us in creation the added fire of a new anointing. We are each empowered to fulfil our human potential when the Sprit's gifts are given. For Paul, the language of gifting is a way into spiritual formation. Our journey of faith is a conversation between breath and clay, a dialogue between our human condition and the gifts of God. The discovery, development and deployment of the gifts God has given is the lifelong journey of faith, and a central task of the church. The importance Paul attributes to this process is captured in the goal he suggests for it. It will continue until we all come to maturity, measuring up to "the full and complete standard of Christ".[5]

Paul explicitly links our growth in the Spirit's gifts with the forming of Christ in us. The giftings of the Spirit, for Paul, are far more than a way to make Christian meetings more interesting. They are more than the icing on the cake of Christian spirituality. They are the very substance of the cake itself. Pentecost is God's way of making possible the intimacy with human beings that his heart has ached for since he first saw his two favourite people walking out of his garden. The relationship of an individual believer, and of the wider body of the church, to God the Holy Spirit, is the very essence of the life of faith. Formation is, in this sense, the engine of vocation. As each member of the church discovers and deploys the gifts the Spirit has given them – in the "natural" realm of their humanity and the "supernatural" realm of his subsequent anointing – the body of Christ is built up and comes to maturity.

It is through our growth in the Spirit that our missional engagement is fuelled. What God does in us spills over into what God does through us. More of his light shines out of us because more of his light has broken into us. In formation the Holy Spirit completes us, bringing to vibrant life the potential he has already, in creation, placed in us. We enter into dynamic dialogue with our Creator, discovering in the interface between human and divine the energy we need for transformation. "Here, then, is the divine economy," Simon Ponsonby writes. "The Father sent his Son; the Son sent the Spirit; and the Spirit sends church."[6]

Think About It: The £10,000 lunch

At the heart of a charismystic community is the reality of dependence on God's power. We open ourselves to the Holy Spirit's gifts and anointing because we know that we can achieve nothing without them.

The seeds of this realization are sown by Jesus himself, long before the Pentecost event. The feeding of the five thousand, for example,[7] illustrates the relationship between the resources we offer to God, and the power he adds to them. Here Philip claims[8] that at least 200 denarii would be needed to buy lunch. What is wonderful is that this claim is so accurate. A denarius was a labourer's wages for the day. An equivalent for us might be £50 – eight hours at the minimum wage for adults of £6.08 per hour. So 200 days' wages stacks up to £10,000 today. Depending on how many women and children had joined the 5,000 men present, that's somewhere between £1 and £2 per lunch – a very fair price for a mass-catered picnic meal. Philip is not just pulling a figure out of the air. He's thought about it, and he's quite skilled at estimating catering costs on a large scale. What he proves is this: it can't be done. If all twelve of the disciples were to set to it and go without a day off, they would just about scrape together the £10,000 in a little over two weeks. By then they would have needed to provide the same amount sixteen times over, or else have watched a large crowd starve while waiting. Disaster. The figures just don't stack up. It's beyond us. "Exactly," says Jesus. "Now get these people sitting down. We're going to have us some lunch…"

The figures beautifully illustrates the difference between our calculations and God's. Even if we pool all our resources, and work like slaves without a break, we will not scratch the surface of the task God has given to the church. But if we will surrender the small resource we have, and seek his ways of empowerment, everything can change.

A Gift Economy

The church comes into being around the evident activity of God's Spirit.
Because the Spirit is at work in each person, the contours of God's
mission become visible as gifts are discovered.[1]

Key Text: Ephesians 4:8

That is why the Scriptures say "When he ascended to the heights,
he led a crowd of captives and gave gifts to his people."[2]

Abstract

**Jesus is the King who celebrates his victory by giving gifts
to his people. Gifts given in creation are brought to life in
Pentecostal fire. Gifts given to the church ensure that everyone,
from the least to the greatest, gets equipped.**

In case there is any doubt that the kingdom of God is a gift
economy, centred on the gifts of God the Holy Spirit, Paul the
Hebrew scholar takes liberties with an ancient text to make
his point.

Rabbinic tradition allows for the interpreting of text
through retranslation, and Paul applies the technique here to
Psalm 68. A psalm of royal victory, it pictures the scene in which
a victorious king, enthroned in the land he has conquered,
receives tribute from his new subjects. "When you ascended to
the heights, you led a crowd of captives. You received gifts from
the people, even from those who rebelled against you."[3]

This would be a picture familiar to the ancient world. The
battle is over. Those the king has conquered in battle now become
his loyal subjects. Even those who formerly fought against him
come before him now to pledge allegiance, and they mark their

pledge by bringing gifts – animals and foodstuffs, gold and jewels – whatever it takes to convince their new lord of their loyalty. Paul intentionally links this enthronement scene to the ascension of Jesus; and the gift-giving to Pentecost. But even as he quotes the psalm, he sees that something has changed. At Pentecost the King does not receive gifts from his subjects, he gives gifts to them. And Paul understands that Jesus has reversed the expectations of royalty. Ever the gift-giver, his enthronement is marked not by the receiving of tribute but by the distribution of grace. So Paul translates the psalm in the light of his understanding of Jesus, and quotes: "When he ascended to the heights, he led a crowd of captives and gave gifts to his people."[4]

Jesus is the one who celebrates victory by giving gifts. The battle of the cross and the triumph of the resurrection make possible the gift-giving of Pentecost.

This is what God has been waiting for. This is what prophets have promised over centuries, that a time would come when the human family would once again be able to receive the very Spirit of God. That which stood in the way of such a gift has been swallowed whole – nothing now prevents the outpouring of God's breath once more into human clay. And the mandate of the church – the whole purpose of this gospel adventure – is to extend and explore the fullness of God's gift-giving spree, bringing more and more human lives to the place where the gifts given in creation can be enlivened and reanimated by the gifts given at Pentecost. No wonder Jesus told his first followers that "it is best for you that I go away"[5] – his "going away" in the ascension triggers the torrent of gift-giving.

The gospel experience, then, is a story of the giving and receiving of gifts. It is about discovering and accepting and enjoying all the gifts that God is giving: about bringing the whole breadth of our lives and experience under the gift-shower of the Holy Spirit until our human journey sparkles with the light of

God. All of us, Paul claims, are gift-receivers. To all of us God gives and for all of us he has purpose. Formation and vocation are the bread-and-butter business of the church because the life of faith is all about discovering my gifts and the purpose for which they were given.

To further explain the workings of this gift economy, Paul identifies three distinct expressions of God's gift-giving. He has begun already in creation, pointing to works "planned for us long ago".[6] In Acts 17, as we have seen, he speaks of God as the one who "gives life and breath to everything",[7] the one in whom "we live and move and have our being".[8] Our very existence, in this light, flows from the generosity of a gift-giving God. The implication is that every human being has gifts and purpose: the very act of breathing is a celebration of God's gifts. Salvation, in this light, is the activation of God's gifts and the actualization of the purpose for which they are given. To be "born again" is to discover why you were born in the first place.

Secondly, Paul refers to the gifts that are given to believers as an outworking of the ascension of Christ: "he has given each one of us a special gift…"[9] All those who make up the *ekklesia* – the gathered expression of human beings choosing to follow Christ – have received gifts. This is in effect the "second gifting" of Pentecost, by which the Creator revisits, in redemption, those he has made. It is impossible to read the theology of Paul without capturing the "all" of this gift-giving. Over and over the body-wide distribution of God's gifts is highlighted, and the goal of the church is made clear: it is that all should come to maturity; that all should thrive; that all might enjoy and express their giftings; that all can live a life of purpose. Whatever God wants for any one of us, he wants for all of us: and the last, the least and the lost feature high on his "desire to bless" lists.

Thirdly, Paul names a number of specific gifts and describes them as given "to the church"[10] – apostles, prophets, evangelists, pastors and teachers. These gifts are not singled out to excuse a kind of back-door elitism, as if Paul has signed up to George Orwell's mantra in *Animal Farm* that "all are equal but some are more equal than others". What sets these gifts apart is that they are given so that all the other gifts can flourish. It is for their necessity, not their status, that these gifts make the cut. The apostles, prophets, evangelists, pastors and teachers are not more important than any other of God's gifted people, but they are needed in order for all God's people to grow. In God's gift economy there are processes that are vital if all God's people are going to discover, develop and deploy their gifts. As we have suggested already, the terms "formation" and "vocation" capture the heart of these processes. It is the calling of leaders in God's church to ensure that formation and vocation are happening across the body of Christ. The church-based gifts exist entirely "to equip God's people".[11]

This is the clearest statement anywhere of the purpose for which leaders are given to the church – and it is dynamite. It tells us that the only goal of leadership is to equip. Enabling people to discover their gifts and empowering them to deploy them are the core business to which all church leaders are called.

This in turn tells us that God's goals for his church can be fully met through the equipping of God's people: if all the leaders given to the church are called to a ministry of equipping, then whatever the church will achieve will be achieved through equipping. And since Paul has already established that it is through the church that the Creator intends to display his wisdom to the cosmos, we are drawn to a single, central, strategy-shaping conclusion: the kingdom will come through equipping, or it will not come at all. This is Plan A, and there is no other. All the goals of the mission of God will be met through the equipping of the people of God. The gifts that are given to leaders are there for the perfection of the gifts that are given to the body. The empowerment of the pulpit is given solely for the empowerment of the pew. Whatever specific tasks are included in the five distinct roles of leaders in the church, however differently the different denominations and styles of church express these details, they are all tasks to be fulfilled in the equipping of God's people.

Equipping – which we have here expressed in the specific categories of formation and vocation – is the engine of God's mission in the world.

Think About It: The "down and out" church

Patterns matter to us. Things we do often, especially where rhythms and rituals are repeated, form a kind of graphic background to our lives. Where patterns have been etched by past behaviours, our default is to follow them.

There is a pattern to our worship and the life of our churches that has been normative to us for so many years, and is etched so deeply in our culture that it will take huge effort to break it. It is the pattern of "in and up" worship. Unconsciously, we see church as an "in and up" experience – we "gather in" our time and energy, our resources and the fruits of our lives, and we "offer them up" to God. The "in and up" movement has its roots in genuine worship, and should indeed be part of our lives. But it is not the whole story. There is also, in the kingdom, a "down and out" movement. The blessings and gifts of God come down on us from heaven. They bless others as we are pushed out into the world. This is the original pattern of the church. It is the shape of Pentecost. It is how there came to be a church in Philippi and Ephesus and Rome. It is why any of us were allowed to join in in the first place.

We've lost the pattern. Our worship services, our ministry programmes, our plans and projects – all too often they conform to an "in and up" movement. We are called to be a "down and out" people: to participate in the coming of God's kingdom by receiving and distributing his blessings. Are you queuing in the

Departure Lounge, passport in hand, or waiting at Arrivals for the kingdom? What good news is God trying to get "down and out" through your life? What shape lies at the heart of your church life?

Honoured Architects

*The leadership gifts given directly to the body of the church
are given so that other, wider gifts are found and used in the body
of the church. As church we participate in equipping one another –
the goal is that all will be equipped.*[1]

Key Text: John 13:14

*Since I, your Lord and Teacher, have washed your feet, you ought to
wash each other's feet.*[2]

Abstract

**All God's gifts are given to empower us to give. Just as Jesus sets
aside his right to tribute and chooses, instead, to bless others, so
we are called to exercise our giftings with such love. The Spirit
empowers us to live for others.**

Paul's insistence that those called to lead in the church are, in
effect, called to serve, carries forward the same switch in polarity
that he has highlighted in the citing of Psalm 68.

Just as Jesus sets aside his right to receive tribute and
chooses instead to give gifts, so those called to leadership are
asked to set aside their sense of privilege or entitlement and
to use their power to bless others. If the gift you have received
is that of leadership, you have received it for the benefit of
others.

In fact, this principle runs throughout the gift economy.
Everything God gives us is for the love and service of others.
All our gifts, it turns out, come alive when surrendered in love
for the sake of others. The gifts of God are given to be given
away. They are not treasure to be hoarded, but currency to

spend on behalf of others, both within and beyond the borders of the church. In this connection, as so often, the words of the prophet Isaiah ring out over the New Testament church: "if you spend yourselves on behalf of the hungry and satisfy the needs of the oppressed, then your light will rise..."[3] God gives us resources not to spend on ourselves, but to fuel us as we spend ourselves for others. His every gift is given to empower us to live for others.

This radical discovery turns the church upside-down and inside-out. It turns the church upside-down because those who appear to be "at the top" of our gatherings are, it turns out, vastly less important than those who seem to be "at the bottom". The leaders are the investors – but the members of the body are the investment. Leadership is a means towards a goal, and the goal is in the wider body of the people of God. The architect of a building may be honoured. Her name may even be inscribed by the front door. But it is not the architect we live in – it is the building. The building is what matters. It is the beauty that your leadership gift produces in the lives of others that gives it lasting value. The gift itself, without such fruit, is little more than a shiny toy. Just as God, the great artist, wants to be known by his art, so leaders are asked to rejoice not in their achievements and successes, but in the glorious achievements of those they lead.

This also turns the church inside-out because it reverses the polarity of our resources. The purpose of gathering, rather than being to concentrate the resources of the people of God – bringing the tithes into the storehouse – is in fact to equip for dispersal. The flow of resources is reversed. Just as Jesus celebrates enthronement not by receiving tributes but by giving gifts, so the church exists not to receive the offerings of God's people but to distribute the gifts of God. The church ceases to be an institution that gathers in the resources of God's people (money; time; effort; energy and vision) so that great things can be achieved. Instead it becomes a movement that pours out resources into its members, to carry into the commerce of their daily lives. Organization is still needed; gathering still matters. There remains a place for giving and volunteering and investing in the institution: but only in the full knowledge that the institution exists for dispersal. Monday to Saturday do not exist to make Sunday wonderful: Sunday exists to make the weekdays fly. Perhaps we need to rediscover Jesus' admonition to the Jews: "the Sabbath was made for man, not man for the Sabbath".[4]

What would it mean for our churches if every gift were evaluated in terms of its capacity to bless others? What would happen if the very functioning of church was reoriented around this chain of giving: from Jesus himself showering us with the Holy Spirit, to leaders seeing every gift they have received as an opportunity to give and serve, and members of Christ's body recognizing that whatever they receive is given so that they can give to others... What kind of world would such a structure give birth to? Might it be a world not unlike Jesus' description of the kingdom:

> *The Kingdom of Heaven is like a mustard seed planted*
> *in a field. It is the smallest of all seeds, but it becomes the*
> *largest of garden plants; it grows into a tree, and birds*
> *come and make nests in its branches.*[5]

The equipping Paul speaks of in Ephesians 4:12 has an unusual dimension to it. In Matthew 4:21 the same word is used to describe the mending of fishing nets. Elsewhere in Greek literature it refers to the resetting of a broken bone. It is about health and preparedness; about being given the inner strength and capacity to live as God asks us to live. Our participation in the body of Christ "mends" us until we are fit for the purpose God has for us, to love and serve our fellow human beings and care for God's non-human creation. This matters because so many of us feel unable to love selflessly. We want to "live for others" but fear we don't have what it takes to do so. Gifted or not, we do not know how to lay down our lives for others.

So the Holy Spirit, through the body of the church, equips us – not only with the gifts and resources we need to do God's work, but with the inner drives and attitudes without which we will fail, swallowed up in our own selfishness. God equips me not only to do what he has asked me to do but to be the person he has called me to be. His goal for my life is that my best self should triumph; that my petty temptations and foolish longings might be overcome, and my small ambitions burnt; that I might surrender to the dream of life lived well and love fully expressed and experienced. The Holy Spirit addresses directly my God-given desire to be a better person.

To be prismatic is to understand this desire at the heart of human existence. I was not created to be a neutral presence in the world – drawing resources of food and water but giving nothing in return. I was not made to pass through unnoticed. I was made for significance; for fruitfulness. My desire is to leave the world in a more beautiful condition than that in which I found it. I want my presence in the world, no matter how brief, to mean something – to others; to my own heart; to the creatures, animate and inanimate, who watch over my progress and are touched by it for better or worse.

Think About It: Coal or diamonds?

How are you equipping others?

The question should underlie every other question about roles of leadership. Leaders exist entirely for this purpose. The whole human adventure is, at root, about discovering, developing and deploying the gifts our Creator has given us. Helping others on this journey – until they shine with such bright beauty that we all start wearing shades around them – is what leadership is for.

When you meet someone new, do you notice first how inadequate they are, or do you start to tingle almost instantly with how incredible they might be? Do you notice the ninety-eight areas in which a person has failed, or focus on the two areas in which they have a thrilling future? If you lead a group of people in an organization or church, how often do you remind yourself of their potential? Are they a heap of coal – black, dusty, useful only for burning? Do you need a sackful of them to generate any energy at all? Or are they diamonds – each shining with an iridescent light; each valuable beyond imagination? Both are rocks – but the way you treat them is not the same! The great thing about diamonds is that just a few of them can change your life forever. What does it mean, in leadership, to move from dealing with quantities of coal to working with the qualities of diamonds?

In the Bless Network we have expressed this passion for the value in each person as a prayer, "God Sees Diamonds":

We believe every human being
has a worth worth seeing
Every name
Is a sound worth saying
Your potential
A prayer worth praying
You see coal – God sees diamonds

We believe in the grace
Of the gifts God gives
His breath
In everything that lives
Greater gifts to be discovered
Deep in you; disguised; dust-covered
You see coal – God sees diamonds

We see God seeking
A servant generation
Kindness as the kindling
To kick-start transformation
Love as liberation
of a captive creation
We are digging
for the diamonds God sees[6]

Task #4: Improvisation

Tom Wright, the former Bishop of Durham, has given the church the great phrase "faithful improvisation". Knowing God's story as it has unfolded thus far and trusting his character and presence to shape our future, we improvise the next chapter in our own time and context. And our improvisations respond directly to the evident actions of God's Spirit. It is as we see the Spirit at work that we are free to improvise. Mission is a dance in which we partner with God.

The book of Acts captures this model well. It is both the Acts of the Apostles and the Acts of the Holy Spirit. The church does not lead the Holy Spirit into mission, but rather follows where the Holy Spirit leads. In Acts 10 Peter finds the Holy Spirit active among Gentile believers. In Acts 16 the apostles gather to discern together the direction the Spirit is leading them in. In Acts 17 Paul is surprised to find the Spirit at work in pagan Athens. Throughout the book, the church pursues a dance in which the Spirit is the lead partner.

Just as the Holy Spirit is forming Christ in each one of is, he is forming the church in the world. The form of the church emerges as the contours of God's mission become clear: in every case because the Spirit is in dialogue with human culture.

We do not lead God into mission. We follow. But neither

do we dance alone. God the Holy Spirit, our partner, lover and friend, is with us, rejoicing as the dance unfolds, step by step to the healing of our world.

God's Brilliant Idea #3:
"Help Them Love!"

The church as a transformant task force

transformation (ˌtransfərˈmā sh ən)

Noun: a thorough or dramatic change in form or appearance; a metamorphosis during the life-cycle of an animal; in physics, the induced or spontaneous change of one element into another; in biology, the genetic alteration of a cell by introduction of extraneous DNA; the heritable modification of a cell from its normal state to a malignant state.
Origin: late Middle English; from Old French, or late Latin *transformatio(n-)*, from the verb *transformare* (see **transform**).

transformant (ˌtransˈfȯr-mənt)

Noun: a cell that has been genetically altered through the uptake of foreign DNA.
Adjective: shaped by the changes God wants and is bringing in me; engaging with change God is bringing to my world.

Transformant Task Force

We are none of us finished
None done
We are half baked
Half built
Half beautiful
Creator God, continue us
Craft us to completion[1]

Key Text: Colossians 1:9–10

We ask God to give you complete knowledge of his will and to give you
spiritual wisdom and understanding. Then the way you live will always
honor and please the Lord, and your lives will produce every kind of
good fruit.[2]

Abstract

**The church comes into being as individuals receive the salvation
God has offered them in Christ. But receiving is not the end of
the story. Recipients are turned outwards to a world in need, and
become part of God's movement for change in the world.**

Slavonski Brod is a jewel of a town in the Slavonia region of
Croatia. "Brod" means "ship" in modern Croatian, but in earlier
times it had the sense of "water crossing" – akin to the English
"ford". Its place in the town's name reflects its most prominent
feature, the Sava: a wide and winding river used for transport
and popular with fishermen, canoeists and promenade-walkers.
It is impossible to miss the river, so important is it to the town's

history and architecture. Slavonski Brod was also the scene of intense fighting in the recent Balkan wars, and the beautiful river no longer simply flows through the town: it divides it between two nations. The bridge has become an international border between Croatia and Bosnia-Herzegovina. The area of the town on the south bank, now called Bosanski Brod, belongs to the Serbian enclave within Bosnia.

So fierce was the fighting at the height of the war that at one stage it was reported that every window in the centre of Slavonski Brod had been broken. This one provincial town played out in miniature the entire crisis of the Balkan nations. Over the past nine years we have had the privilege, through the Bless Network, of taking teams of young people into Brod each summer. Working in partnership with the Baptist church there, we run sports camps and children's clubs, and an evening "youth space". The aim is to offer unconditional love and unrestrained encouragement to the children and young people of the town. Many have been born since peace broke out: but there are none who are not in some way marked by war. Every family has been touched by the devastation that swept through the region in the 1990s. Many continue to be touched by the economic uncertainties of a stop–start recovery.

We have seen our teams make a measurable impact on the town and we have regular contact with many of the local young people they have worked with. But something else has happened that we didn't expect, and are immeasurably grateful for. Slavonski Brod has made an impact on our teams. Something about being in this place so recently traumatized, bringing words of hope and encouragement to children and teens, speaking blessing over them, has deeply affected the hearts of the young people who have made up our teams. We challenge our teams not only to act but also to pray. We ask them to worship God in the open air, seeking his heart for the city. We urge them to grasp and hold onto a vision for this city God so loves. And the starkness of this context has enabled many to come to a deeper understanding of the mission of God.

When we visited the team in July 2011, we joined them on the riverbank, where they were taking time to pray for the town. They sang in worship and brought to God their hopes and dreams for this broken city. Chalks were distributed, and the team began to write their prayers on the riverside pavement. In coloured chalks, the words in places decorated with cartoon crowns and flowers, they wrote on the skin of Slavonski Brod:

> *"A crown of beauty instead of ashes"*
> *"More valuable than a whole flock of sparrows"*
> *"Turning brokenness into beauty"*
> *"God will paint grace graffiti on the fences. All the frightened children will run to him"*

What does it mean to write such words on the pavements of a town you are growing to love? Does such an act have meaning beyond the moment? Our sense is that in the lives of these young people it does. Those writing were young adults, mostly from the UK. None of them would claim to have a sophisticated or well-developed missiology. They would not present themselves as experts in the things of God. But what they do have is a hunch. It is a hunch that the God who is at work in their lives and in the lives of others around also has a dream for towns and cities: that the God who created every person in Slavonski Brod has dreams for each of their lives. They have a hunch that God's work in the world is about change – change for the better and change for good.

Nearly 2,000 kilometres north, in Lisieux in France, our teams have worked in a similar way on Hauteville, a public housing area with 9,000 residents and many issues around drugs, crime and gang culture. Lisieux is a cathedral city and one of the most established pilgrimage centres in France. After

Lourdes, more spiritual seekers come to the city of "La Petite Therese" than to any other French shrine. But Lisieux is also a city of high unemployment, with a local economy rocked by changes in French agricultural and industrial life. Many families struggle with the social issues related to low incomes, poor educational achievement and limited opportunity: and many such issues find their focus in Hauteville.

The commitment of our teams has been to pray for the area and to work alongside children and young people, bringing whatever joy they can and seeking to bless the families of the area. On one of their early expeditions to the area, our teams wrote prayers of blessing on the soles of their shoes, walking them across the Hauteville turf. When they checked later in the day, the prayers were gone: worn off as the day wore on. They were struck by the serendipity of this event, sensing that their prayers had been deposited on the ground they walked. They now write sole blessings every time they visit.

What these young people have come in some small way to grasp is that the mission of God is, at heart, a work of transformation. That which God does in me he wants to do in the wider world. There is a qualitative link between the inner transformation I experience in Christ and the outward transformation he will bring to whole communities. We can walk the blessings of God into the dust of Hauteville and pray for a crown of beauty for Slavonski Brod because we believe that ultimately this is what God wants. Where war has brought trauma and devastation, the God of peace longs to bring repair. Where enmity has torn down walls and raised up fences, the God of reconciliation longs for grace to do its work. The gospel we proclaim is a message of transformation, and there is no outer limit to how far God would have that transformation be known.

Throughout the New Testament a link is made between the inward, personal work of salvation associated with the cross and the outward flow of transformation that will ultimately renew the cosmos itself.

- In Ephesians 1 Paul lists the many blessings delivered for the believer through the work of Christ. He describes a God who loves us and chooses us and brings us into his family; a God rich in grace and kindness who sets us free. But this same God has a plan to do much more than this. He will ultimately bring everything under the authority of Christ; things both on earth and in heaven. He will bring Jews and non-Jews together to share a remarkable inheritance.[3]
- In Colossians 1 Paul rejoices that the new believers of Colossae are the fruit of the gospel and then prays that they will bear the fruits of the gospel.[4]
- In his letter to the Christians of Rome, Paul spends paragraph after paragraph outlining what it is that God has done in Christ for the believer, and then calls every believer to live a life of sacrifice that is the only reasonable response. "Let God transform you into a new person by changing the way you think," he says. "Then you will learn to know God's will for you, which is good and pleasing and perfect."[5]

In each of these admonitions there is a pattern linking inward and outward transformation. The New Testament does not see us as passive recipients of salvation – those who are changed by the work of Christ. Rather, it invites us into active participation in God's plans to bring salvation to the world – to be those who, changed by the work of Christ, become agents of change in their world. It pops and fizzes with the life of God, infusing culture like a soluble aspirin. It brings change by its very nature, and the more its members surrender to the transforming presence of God, the more change it brings. Changed people change people, and the people they change change the world. Those called to inward transformation are turned outward to their neighbour in loving service. Those receiving forgiveness are empowered to forgive. Those transformed by grace become the very essence of grace to others. The people of God are called not only to receive healing but to be a source of healing in their world; not only to know reconciliation but to bring reconciliation; not only to be blessed but to carry blessing outward. The church that is formed as a result of God's movement of change in the world by turn becomes God's movement for change in the world.

The fruit becomes the seed to bear more fruit. Those whose lungs have been cleansed by breathing in the pure mountain air of grace breathe out that same grace air into their smog-bound world. For the New Testament there can be no receiving without giving; no being forgiven that does not also forgive. The Christian story emerges in our world and reshapes our experience because it transforms the lives into which, as a seed, it is embedded. That which is emerging in the world is also emerging in me. The kingdom of God is coming into being around me and is also what I am becoming. Personal, relational, social and ultimately global change grow from this seed of transformation. Without personal change there is no hope for global transformation. Without global vision there is no purpose for personal change. The two are interlinked, drawing on the same resources and driven by the same transforming narrative, dispelling darkness wherever God's light is brought to bear.

The promise of Isaiah is that the people who surrender to God's call to love others will be like a well-watered garden. And they will also rebuild the walls of their city. A prismatic faith is by definition transformant, bringing change to the very genome of human community. We are sent into the world not to rescue people from it, but to bring to it all the change that grace can bring. The church is a transformant task force.

Think About It: Hungry for heaven

Watching the BBC transmission of Coldplay at Glastonbury 2011 was mesmerizing. To see thousands of people singing the gospel-inspired "Fix you", a sea of hands in the air... there is only one word to describe such a moment. It was worship. Back in 1995 poet Steve Turner wrote *Hungry for Heaven – Rock 'N Roll and the Search for Redemption,*[6] developing the thesis that popular music is ultimately religiously driven. If you need proof that music is born of a longing for the divine, one evening at Glastonbury offered it. What do people think they are reaching for, as they stretch their hands to the sky? Probably a thousand different things: as many different creeds and credulities as there are people in the crowd. But somewhere at the root of each longing is the same God-given dream. That the world can be as it should be. That beauty is possible. That love lives. Music may not hold the answer to such longings, but it is the loudest, the strongest, the most aching means we have of asking the questions.

Task #5: Imagination

We have had cause on several occasions on this journey to talk about imagination. We have called for a vision of the church to inspire the imaginations of our culture, perhaps especially of the rising generation. We have seen that God calls us to be imaginative, and promises to exceed our every longing. But is there a deeper sense in which imagination is a task of the church?

Too often in our churches imagination is associated with creativity and the arts, and not with the everyday business of being church. We assume that only "creatives" need to be imaginative. But in practice mission doesn't work this way. The phase of imagination is a vital bridge between the way things are now and the way God wants them to be. When we begin to see what God wants and, knowing that it isn't yet delivered, hunger for it with every fibre of our being, that which lives in our imagination begins to bear fruit in reality.

As Gregory Boyd has shown, prayer and the imagination can be creative and dynamic partners.[7] Boyd has criticized the evangelical tendency to assume "everybody who advocates the use of imagination in prayer to be part of a New Age conspiracy trying to take over the church".[8] He has taught widely on the linking of prayer with the imagination. He finds a strong precedent for this in Christian devotional history, and suggests that imagination is increasingly "acknowledged by scientists as foundational for thinking and emotions".[9]

Imagination is essential in praying for the missional call of the church because it steps in, by definition, to the space between what is and what can be. Where else does prayer belong except in the space of longing for the will of God to be done?

Can our churches become engine-rooms of the imagination, forging and fuelling the imaginative visions that will lead us all to long for, and work for, God's coming kingdom?

Rooted and Booted

Being shaped by God's presence. Being fuelled by his power. Being formed for his purposes. These are the adventures God calls us to in his church. If we will accept his invitation, we will never be the same again – and neither will our world.[1]

Key Text: John 15:5

Yes, I am the vine; you are the branches. Those who remain in me, and I in them, will produce much fruit. For apart from me you can do nothing.[2]

Abstract

The Spirit who calls us to inward change also calls us to outward engagement. The one who enables our intimacy with God empowers our service in God's world. The deeper in we dive into the life of the Spirit, the further out God will call us in service.

We noted earlier the importance of Jesus' description of the church as a vine, bringing together the opposite movements of being "drawn in" and "sent out".

This comes centre stage in the transformant adventure of the church. We are invited inwards towards the cultivation of intimacy with God; into the place of prayer and encounter; into nakedness before our Creator, and we are urged outwards towards engagement with our world; towards culture and service and mission and wrestling for the kingdom to come. Maintaining the dynamic tension between these two imperatives, holding us accountable for both inner growth and outward fruitfulness, is one of the key tasks of the community of faith.

God calls us to be rooted and booted. To put our roots deep down into Christ, taking the time needed to grow in relationship with him and opening ourselves to the probing, prodding light of the Holy Spirit in our hearts. But to know, also, that there will be a time to be booted; equipped for mission, ready to engage for God's purposes in God's world. We come to the sacred place of prayer and hear the words, "Take off your shoes." Do we also hear the words that follow: "Put on your boots"?

All too often churches make a choice between these two. Seeing the need for depth in discipleship, we emphasize the inward call of Christ and overprivatize our faith. Or seeing the needs of the world, we abandon prayer and privacy and plunge head-first into our culture, seeking purpose. Paul's prayer for his Ephesian friends seeks energy in both directions. He prays for them that "Christ will make his home in your hearts as you trust in him. Your roots will grow down into God's love and keep you strong."[3] But this is not the end of his dream for them. Rooted in this way in Christ, he prays further that they will "have the power to understand, as all God's people should, how wide, how long, how high and how deep his love is".[4]

The first is a call to rootedness, the second to limitless adventure. In the width and length and height and depth of God's love is contained all of his desire for the healing of the world. Every starving child. Every acid-scarred tree. Every life destroyed and distorted by anger and addiction and abuse. Every human cry of lostness. Every bleeding wound of the damage we have done to God's world. All these are included in the boundless, bottomless, endless love of God. To press into his presence is to discover this love. To bathe in his beauty is to be soaked in such mercy. The deeper we dive into him, the further we find ourselves thrust out into his broken world. Rooted, we find ourselves booted. Drawn in, we find ourselves sent.

In his letter to the Romans Paul graphically depicts this connection between prayer and action. The longing of the created order for the liberation made possible in Christ is so strong, Paul says, that it is as if the world is "groaning as in the pains of childbirth".[5] And we, in a similar way, long for our own liberation, to be released from sin and suffering. And as we pray, engaging with the Spirit of the God who made not only us but the very fabric of the world we walk through, we are drawn to dream his dream of a world made new. We press deep into God's longings for the world, and when his desire in us runs beyond the end of the words we can find for it, we hear within ourselves the Holy Spirit praying "with groanings that cannot be expressed in words".[6]

Around us, a world groans for change, longing for the liberation that words cannot express. Within us, the Holy Spirit echoes that cry, birthing in us the very longings of creation. The place of prayer, of our encounter with God, does not take us away from the world's needs, but deeper into them.

Part of our responsibility as the people of God is to foster these places of radical encounter; where meeting God by his Spirit and embracing his dream for the world come together. We are called to establish a rhythm as fluid as breathing, moving seamlessly between the promises of God and the needs of a broken world, soaking our own souls in his presence and bathing the wounds of the poor by his love. If our encounter with the Spirit of God seems to take us away from the world he loves, we should ask ourselves how this has come to be. If our engagement with God's world draws away from knowing him, we should ask the same. God is forming us by his Spirit in the way of Christ, whose intimacy with the Father neither interfered with nor was threatened by time spent with prostitutes and sinners.

The Spirit who made us is the Spirit who anoints us for service. The Spirit who enables our intimacy with God is the

Spirit who empowers us for engagement. The Spirit whose presence we seek in prayer is present already in the world. We do not lead him, we follow. We do not bring him to the poor, we find him with them.

Think About It: Blessing

As we journey towards transformation – of our own inner lives and of our world – we never journey alone. God is with us. His story shapes us. He dreamed of us centuries before we were born. He dreams, still, of the future he has called us to. This poem is a blessing calling on the Father, Son and Spirit to journey with each one of us. As you consider God's transforming work in your own heart, and look to all he calls you to, can you make this your prayer?

Blessing

May God in whose furnace
Faith is forged;
In whose being
Beauty breathes;
From whose dawning
Darkness flees,

Shine on you

May the Father whose love for you
Beats with a rhythm time itself can't stop
Whose presence in your exile
Is the promise of home
Whose certainties are deeper
Than the cellars of your city
Whose breath is life

Breathe on you

May the Son whose story
Is a mirror of your own
Who has journeyed into darkness
To find a key to your prison
Who has dived the deepest oceans
To find pearls for your wisdom
Who has looked into your heart
And found a beauty worth the battle
Who has written your name
On a white stone carved in secret

Hold you

May the Spirit who has waited
Millennia to fill you
Who shaped the word
That moved the wind
Of the morning that conceived you
Who holds the earth
On which you stand
As an artist holds a candle
Who fully knows you:

Wholly own you

So may God,
The faithful Father,
God the scarred Son,
God the sculpting Spirit
Journey with you[7]

Think About It: Between sea and sky

One of the places I visit most consistently – at least once a year, more often when it's possible – is Quiberon, a peninsula off the south coast of Brittany. It is in visiting this place that I am most often able to put my own life in perspective: and to see the sometimes grasping and often fearful motivations that hide under my need for a lifestyle of comfort.

I find it hard to describe the emotions I experience in this former tidal island, now linked to mainland France by a single road. It is for me a "thin place" unlike any other. The wilder western coast of the peninsula, a riot of caves and coves constantly beaten by a hungry sea, pushed my understanding, this year, of landscape and prayer. The two most powerful presences here are the sea and the sky: where the land intrudes it is only to give structure to the immensity of the other two. It is by definition a place of borders, where the box-like houses we build to give expression to the small ambitions of our tiny lives are utterly dwarfed by the breadth of their surroundings.

The weather is everything here, driving an ocean that can plunge from benevolence to malevolence with a simple change of the wind's direction. Every home has shutters, and every shutter has to be repainted yearly: our efforts at self-protection and style-projection are mocked by the power of the elements. It is impossible not to sense the scale of things. I am made aware at one and the same time of the smallness of my existence and of the immensity of love that frames me. To name the planet "God" is pantheism… to let the planet call God's name to me is worship.

Task #6: Imitation

If imagination is the task by which the church enters into the "now but not yet" of God's kingdom, acknowledging that

God's will is not done but praying that it will be, then imitation is the task by which God's kingdom comes. It is as we live the life of Jesus, acting as Jesus would act and treating people as Jesus would treat them, that a kingdom culture will emerge around us.

Jesus was called, once for all as the incarnate Son of God, to embody God's kingdom in a human life. Those he touched were touched by the kingdom. Those he spoke to heard the words of the kingdom. Those he loved and accepted received the unconditional welcome characteristic of the kingdom. Jesus embodied the kingdom banquet that his parables so often described. His very life was a party for the purposes of God. Our calling is not to repeat this – the incarnation of Christ is, by definition, a unique event. But as we walk in imitation of Christ, living as he lived and speaking as he spoke, we will embody that same kingdom. We are called, each one of us, to the imitation of Christ.

Crucially, it is not as individuals that we will embody Jesus. It is the church that is the body of Christ, not the individual believer. We each make a contribution, pouring love out in a thousand acts of kindness, but it is together that we are Jesus' body.

What would a body made up of people who each walk in imitation of Christ look like? How do we fulfil our corporate calling to imitate Jesus?

Charlie Chaplin's Cane

The call to the church is to be like Jesus; to imitate and emulate his life and ministry. And if there is one word that sums up that life, it is love. Jesus loved in service; loved in teaching and caring; loved in healing and direction and encouragement and joy. His every action was qualified by love. And he calls us to follow this same path.[1]

Key Text: Philippians 2:3–5

Never act from motives of rivalry or personal vanity, but in humility think more of each other than you do of yourselves. None of you should think only of his own affairs, but should learn to see things from other people's point of view. Let Christ himself be your example as to what your attitude should be.[2]

Abstract

In his incarnation Jesus touched those in need around him. Healing and blessing came to many, and good news was announced to the poor. As the body of Christ in the world today, we are called to do the same. The church is a movement of servant love.

The American author Anne Rice, born in 1941, is one of the world's most celebrated and best-selling writers of Gothic fiction. Best known for her series The Vampire Chronicles, which includes *Interview with the Vampire* (1976), *The Queen of the Damned* (1988), and *Merrick* (2000), Rice has recently returned to the Christian faith of her childhood, and has begun a series of seven novels recording "the autobiography of Jesus".

The first volume of the series, *Christ the Lord: Out of Egypt*,[3] is a fictionalized account of the childhood of Jesus, beginning with his family's return to Nazareth from Egypt, where they have lived in exile since fleeing Herod's massacre of the innocents. The book focuses on Jesus' gradual realization of his identity and power as God's Messiah. The follow-up, *The Road to Cana*,[4] takes Jesus to the very moment when his career as a travelling rabbi is launched. In both volumes Rice displays her trademark commitment to research and historic detail, making the most of recent scholarship to create a compelling and believable portrayal. Her search, she has said, is for the authentic Jesus.

In her spiritual memoir, *Called out of Darkness*, Rice explains how she came to have such a desire to understand not only the divinity but also the humanity of Jesus. Describing herself as a "Christmas Christian" rather than an "Easter Christian", she speaks of the birth of Jesus as the central and most perfect miracle of all:

> *This [the incarnation] is not merely the measure of love,*
> *but the measure of an overwhelming affirmation of the*
> *human condition. You have been a child, so I become a*
> *child. That seems to be what the Infant in Mary's arms*
> *is saying to me. No wonder he can later say with such*
> *conviction in Matthew 18: "Unless you turn and become*
> *like children, you will not enter the Kingdom of Heaven."*
> *He had become a child, quite literally and completely, to*
> *enter the Kingdom of Humankind.*[5]

For Rice, faith is all about incarnation. Derived from the Latin term for "flesh" – *caro*, as used in "carnivore", "carnal" and "carnival" – incarnation speaks of being "in flesh". To get a sense of the depth of this word, consider the meaning of related words in current usage. The clearest derivative of the term in contemporary culture is in chilli con carne, meaning literally "chillies with meat". In incarnation Jesus comes to us as God con carne: God in meat. The Creator is fully embodied in the flesh of one of his own creatures. This is a radical proposition to the Jewish mind because God is the one who is, by definition, without flesh. He is above and beyond the created world. He stands apart from it as its originator and sustainer. "God con carne" is a paradox, as witnessed by the centuries it took for the Christian churches to settle on a theological understanding of Christ's incarnation.

But for the New Testament writers, incarnation is more than a one-off paradox conveniently delivering the Son of God to the earth: it is a resounding affirmation of God's commitment to humanity. By adopting and fully indwelling the human condition, Jesus enacts the Creator's loving endorsement of the human race. He embodies God's original ambition, to express his love and wisdom for the creation through human lives. Jesus makes it possible for humanity once again to stand in God's intended place in his creation: and then he issues the most cosmos-changing invitation of all. He invites us to follow him.

Theologians are divided as to how appropriate it is to speak of the church continuing the incarnation of Christ. In so many senses incarnation is a unique event. It is the central miracle of our faith in which the invisible God takes on flesh. We cannot follow in this because we are, by definition, flesh already. But as Paul so beautifully expresses it in Philippians 2, the incarnation represents a way of being that we can follow. It is a move from power to powerlessness[6] and from distance to proximity. It involves a setting aside of privilege to identify with the underprivileged.[7] It is an act of "self-emptying", and it is in this sense that we are called to follow. We cannot reproduce Christ's incarnation, but we can live with the same attitude.[8]

Perhaps the most useful term for this act is not incarnation but imitation. We honour the incarnate Christ, and we demonstrate the depth of that honour through our own act of imitation. We are called to emulate Christ's presence in the world.

Imagine arriving in a seaside town for a weekend break. You've been busy and are tired, and you fall asleep on the train until the jolt of arrival wakes you. You rub your eyes, gather your belongings and disembark from the train. But as you set off on foot to find your hotel, you wonder if you might still be dreaming. You pass Charlie Chaplin in the ticket hall, and then again, miraculously, holding the door for you as you leave. Just outside the Post Office he waddles by again and outside your hotel there are four Charlies unloading gear from a white Transit van. You think you may have crossed into a parallel universe, until you realize you have in fact walked into a lookalike convention. You work this out slowly in your tiredness, but in the end the moustaches, the little hats, the walking-canes give it away. Why would everybody be dressed like Charlie Chaplin if not for such a convention? Why would people walk like Charlie and behave like Charlie unless looking like Charlie was their thing?

Now imagine a second weekend break, a few months later. Again you are tired. Again you fall asleep on the train. Again the jolt wakes you and you rouse yourself and set off for your hotel. This time, though, the convention is a gathering of Christians. It is followers of Christ, not Charlie Chaplin lookalikes, who have taken over the town. So here's the question: how would you know?

What is it that sets Christians apart, that identifies them? And what is it supposed to be? The answer to the first question might range from stickers and sandals to rainbow guitar-straps. The answer to the second is simpler – it's supposed to be love. Servant love, in the manner of Jesus, is intended to be the mark of the Christian community: as clear and recognizable as Charlie Chaplin's cane and walk. Catholic theologians have called this the "option for the poor" – it is the weighting of the church's mission towards those most in need. Because kindness moves towards those who are suffering, because the mission of God is to free humans from all that distorts his image in them, the calibration of the church around a "kindness revolution" is good news for the poor.

Think About It: Companions in suffering

Compassion is a word that is often spoken but rarely lived. At its root it is about how I feel when I see the sufferings of another. To get to the meaning of true compassion, consider a parallel word – companion. The Latin prefix "com-" is a short form of "common" – it means to share or "have the same as"; "-panion" is derived from the everyday word for bread. So companionship is defined in terms of having the same bread – my companion is "the one I share bread with". Compassion comes about in the same way. The Latin root of passion was not "strong feelings", but "strong suffering" – hence *The Passion of the Christ*. Compassion, then, means shared suffering.

I have compassion when I share the suffering of another – that is, I volunteer to feel what they feel. I surrender my will and allow my (relative) comfort to be coloured by the invasive entry of their (relative) pain. Compassion does not end, of course, in feelings – it flows into action. The bridge between the two is key. If I allow the sufferings of another to affect me as if they were my own, I will tend to act in response, just as I would in dealing with my own pain. If human beings are experts at anything, it is acting to relieve their own pain. When I feel suffering as if it were my own, action in response flows freely.

Compassion, then, is the gift of treating others as I treat myself; of being as shaken by their loss, their hunger, their redundancy as I would be by my own. It challenges the one who is not in pain to share voluntarily a load that another has been forced to carry.

None of us can live constantly and exclusively in this mode – we would be consumed by need and pain. But we can ask for a more compassionate heart; we can make room for compassion; we can ask for the gift of looking less often with indifference. Will we take the opportunities God gives us to move from dispassion ("This means nothing to me") to compassion ("I feel this pain as if it were my own")?

Meekonomics

To be the body of Christ then, is to live-out the principles of Christ's incarnation. In its internal relationships and in its external impact, the church is called to be a community of embodied love – with servanthood and sacrifice written through it like "Brighton" through a stick of rock.[1]

Key Text: Isaiah 11:4

But with righteousness He shall judge the poor,
And decide with equity for the meek of the earth;
He shall strike the earth with the rod of His mouth,
And with the breath of His lips He shall slay the wicked.[2]

Abstract

To live in imitation of a servant King is to enter into a story that subverts our common cultural grasp of wealth and power. The Christian narrative does not come armed with weapons of oppression and control but with the liberating grace of servanthood. Concepts of power and wealth, deeply invested in the human myth of royalty, are utterly subverted by a King who chooses sacrifice. The missional calling of the church is steeped in such servanthood and characterized by self-giving love; our callings are marked and measured by love of God and neighbour. The poor and meek are not mission's victims but its heroes, set to inherit the richest prize of all time.

When Jesus suggested in Matthew 5:5 that "the meek will inherit the earth" he was not speaking into a vacuum. He was citing a tradition that already existed in Hebrew thinking, of God's plans for "the blessed poor". In Psalm 37 we read: "Soon the wicked will disappear. Though you look for them, they will be gone. The lowly will possess the land and will live in peace and prosperity."[3] The Authorized Bible translated this as "the meek will inherit the earth", rightly recognizing that this was the same phrase that Jesus was using. When you move from Hebrew to Aramaic to Greek to English, it's not always easy to keep track, and there was no one with a tape recorder capturing the sermon on the mount. But it is highly likely, when Jesus declared the meek blessed on the basis of the inheritance reserved for them, Psalm 37 was not far from his mind.

Isaiah's words, quoted above, carry the same message. In the NLT these become: "He will give justice to the poor and make fair decisions for the exploited. The earth will shake at the force of his word, and one breath from his mouth will destroy the wicked."[4] There was an expectation among the Jews that the coming Messiah would "put things right", and that this would include two specific actions. Those who are oppressed would have their burdens lifted from them. And those who were oppressing them would no longer be able to do so. Both would be freed from the very different prisons oppression had locked them into.

As part of a series of prayers called *twitturgies*, prayed in the 140-character limit of the Twitter format, I wrote a prayer in 2009 that said:

> *The meek will inherit the earth:*
> *do business with them.*
> *The poor are blessed:*
> *seek blessing among them.*
> *God teach me*
> *the laws of meekonomics.*[5]

I define meekonomics as "the science of living in the world as if the meek really were about to inherit it". The point here is that a world which will ultimately belong to the poor and meek requires a different lifestyle response than a world in which those currently winning in political and economic terms will always do so. In his incarnation Jesus sets aside the greatest level of wealth and power that is even possible – equality with God – in order to take on the lowest position available in the culture into which he had come – death on a cross, showing us by example that the directional flow of the kingdom will be from wealth towards poverty and from power towards the powerless.

The energy of the kingdom is always drawn towards the poor. It always moves towards those in need. The question for us is what this means for the church. How does this polarity or directionality of the kingdom message affect the unfolding of church? If the message of Christ is like a pool-table with one leg shorter than the other three, do we rejoice that the balls keep falling into one corner pocket? Or do we fold a wedge out of the pages of our Bible, prop up the leg, and level things off? The inbuilt desire of human beings to seek wealth and power, and to secure themselves behind walls and fences of economic strength, will mean that the kingdom's tendency to move towards the poor will be resisted. Will our inbuilt tendency to secure our own future drown out in us God's call to fight for the security of others?

The evidence of history suggests that this does happen, and further suggests that the current Western church may have accommodated itself a little too much to the comforts and rewards of our culture. David Smith, in *Mission After Christendom*, suggests that for the Western church, "the question comes to be defined thus: has the acculturation of the churches to a culture shaped by fundamentally materialistic values resulted in the eclipsing of the authentic message of Christ, leaving believers incapable of pointing towards an alternative vision for the future of humankind and the world?"[6]

If David Smith's question is the right one, the implications are deeply challenging. Kingdom living will call for a counter-cultural movement *within* the church so that the church can become once more a counter-cultural movement in society.

A movement that embodies the values of Jesus will move from rich to poor, from powerful to powerless, in every dimension of its life. This will dictate the processes by which we identify and develop leaders in the church; the kinds of "successes" we celebrate in people's lives; the way we respond to people who are broken and struggling; the room we make in our gatherings for those who have not "made it" in the terms set out by consumer culture. It will dictate a new relationship between churches in neighbourhoods and nations of power and influence and those in areas of struggle. It will impact our response to the fragility of our planet. It will place sustainability and solidarity at the very top of our "to do" lists – not as values we reluctantly add to our plans, but as the very core of our vision.

Only such a movement can seriously hope to be a source of healing in the world. How can the church be good news to the poor if it has no contact with them? How can we deliver God's message to the oppressed if we don't have their address?

Imagine you are a small-town lawyer, dealing day to day with the property and inheritance issues of your community. One day a stranger comes into your office with a job for you. He explains that an old lady has died and, much to everyone's surprise, she was sitting on a fortune valued at multiple millions. Work has been done to trace surviving relatives, and it turns out that the main beneficiary is a woman born and raised in your community. Except that she is thought to now be homeless, and all the authorities have is a name, a description and a rumour that she is still in your town. Your job is to find her, and let her know that she stands to inherit a fortune.

Welcome to the task of the New Testament church. The meek will inherit the earth. Will you accept the job of finding them and telling them?

Think About It: Is enough enough?

The recent conversation about the bonuses paid to senior bankers was extraordinary – to the point of being surreal.

Did anyone outside the rarefied world of global banking even know how things were, before the credit crunch threw a spotlight on these practices?

Can it be true on planet earth that some of these senior employees earn compensation worth 1,000 times the salary of their average colleague, and hundreds of times the salary of some of the world's most significant political leaders?

And that the governments of those same leaders, now also major shareholders in some of the biggest banks, can't do anything to change this situation?

We thought Michael Douglas was being ironic when he said (in the first *Wall Street* movie), "Greed is good", but in 2010 the senior leaders of the world's biggest banks asserted that, without the motivation of greed, no one would work for them. Greed and acquisition are so built-in to the system that to suggest even tempering compensation, in a time of crisis, with a voluntary cap on bonuses was initially received as tantamount to dismantling the banks.

"Ideas have legs," the theologian Al Wolters said several decades ago. Belief systems become political and economic reality, either blessing the poor with bread or depriving them of life itself. We have been failed both by the rigours and excesses of communism and by the unfettered liberties of capitalism. The world has never more urgently needed an economic model that allows for the possibility of personal gain but balances it effectively with solidarity and social responsibility.

Centuries ago, when a ragtag gathering of wandering tribes, recently released from slavery, formed themselves into a nation, they did so on the basis of just such a model. The economic impact of Sabbath and Jubilee went deep and offered to the entrepreneur the freedom to benefit from hard work, and to the poor the security of being protected from destitution. And they did it by the application of a single, simple concept: enough. When you have enough, take a break. Lie fallow for a while. Give some back. Spread the benefits. Give others a chance to achieve their "enough". The laws were complex, but this was their impact: a yes to the motivation that comes from personal gain, but a yes, too, to the right of each new generation to also benefit. The only answer to a rampant bonus culture is: enough is enough.

God's Brilliant Idea #4:
"Make Them One!"

The church as a metanational movement

meta- (ˌmetə)

Combining form: denoting a change of position or condition; denoting position behind, after, or beyond; denoting something of a higher or second-order kind.
Origin: from Greek *meta*, "with, across, or after".

national ('na sh ənəl)

Adjective: of or relating to a nation; common to or characteristic of a whole nation; owned, controlled, or financially supported by the federal government.
Noun: a citizen of a particular country, typically entitled to hold that country's passport.
Origin: late sixteenth-century French, from Latin *natio(n-)*, "birth, race of people" (see **nation**).

metanational- (metə 'na sh ənəl)

Adjective: the fruit of many nations; the property of none.

Metanational Movement

Where we are oceans apart
may God give us
the curiosity of Columbus.
If we are on different planets
grant us God
the boldness of James Kirk.[1]

Key Text: Ephesians 2:17–18

He brought this Good News of peace to you Gentiles who were far away
from him, and peace to the Jews who were near. Now all of us can come
to the Father through the same Holy Spirit because of what Christ has
done for us.[2]

Abstract

**Issues of race and difference were as pressing for the New
Testament church as they are for us today. But facing the
challenge, and pushing through to reconciliation, became
normative for them. The church God is forming is a new human
family, as prismatic in its ethnic make-up as it is in its impact on
the world.**

The awareness campaign "Let's Kick Racism Out of Football"[3]
has set itself the unenviable task of battling abuse and prejudice
in the high-octane world of the sports fan. Football is known
worldwide for its capacity to bring people together. But it can
also be a vehicle for the worst kinds of tribalism. In 2001 the
campaign commissioned a high-profile TV ad to raise awareness
of its cause.[4] Against grainy black-and-white images drawn from
the terraces, and a subdued soundtrack of an orchestra playing

"Land of Hope and Glory", the poet Benjamin Zephaniah narrates his own poem "Dear White Fella". With a rich, deep voice infused with the rhythms of Jamaica, the Handsworth-born poet rejoices in the fact that while black people remain black in all circumstances, white people are born pink and grow up white only to turn variously red (from sunburn), blue (from cold), yellow (in fear), green (in sickness) and grey (in the ashes of death). How ironic is it then, that it is black people who are called "coloured"?

I appreciate this advert for its creativity as well as for its message, and have shown it many times in church weekends and leadership seminars. The tragedy is that often, when I do, I am looking out at an audience that is 100 per cent white. Not just mostly white or predominantly white, but entirely white. Many of the churches of the UK are white enough to offer themselves as models for a washing powder commercial. Whatever changes have come to the ethnic mix of Britain in the past forty years, they have yet to seep into many of our congregations. In the American context of the 1960s, Martin Luther King Jr famously said: "11 o'clock Sunday morning is the most segregated hour of the week... And the Sunday school is still the most segregated school."[5] King realized that far from leading the way to racial integration, the churches were lagging behind. Might he say the same if he toured the UK today? If he visited your church?

The question we must ask is not only whether King's claim would be true of us, but whether, if it is, we should be worried. Is monocultural church just the best way of doing it, an acceptable compromise with human comfort – or is the vision of integration part of the Bible's story? I want to suggest that the latter is and must be true: that bringing diverse peoples together in one body – the one new family of God – is a crucial element of the New Testament church. I believe this is so for three reasons: because it is the right thing to do, because it is the future God is calling us to, and because it makes for a great church! Monocultural churches just don't have the vibrancy and energy of the New Testament community. They offer only part of the picture. Part of what makes the New Testament vision prismatic in the first place is that it brings together people of every shade and shape.

When I took on the leadership of Crossroads International Church in Amsterdam in 2005, my family became part of a community made up of more than forty nationalities. Amsterdam lays claim to being the world's most ethnically diverse city, though the claim is hotly contested and the race is neck-and-neck with New York. Less than half of Amsterdam's population use Dutch as a first language, and even among those who do, English comes a close second. Others come from every part of the world. We worshipped alongside North Americans, but with them were Africans and Surinamese and Malaysians. Chinese bankers recently arrived from communist Beijing were baptized alongside Dutch teenagers and English wanderers who had come to Amsterdam seeking drugs and freedom.

Worshipping in such a community, meeting week by week with people whose skintones ranged from coal to snow and all points in between, changed my faith more deeply than any experience I can remember. I discovered the incredible beauty of a many-coloured family, and the inestimable joy of celebrating life and love in full colour.

The common language of the church was English, which I thought at first might make my life easy. But I discovered some interesting things about language along the way. The English we shared as a multinational community was not, as it turned out, the English of my childhood and education. Rather, it was a new "World English": a fast-spreading language sometimes called Globish. Globish may be growing into the language most common to planet earth: a Latin for the postmodern generation. Founded on English but taking in North American, Asian and other influences, Globish is spoken far more widely as a second language than as a first. For some of the families in the church it wasn't the birth-language of either parent, but was the only language they shared. I found I had as much to learn as anyone to become fluent in this new tongue – especially as a public speaker. A simplified vocabulary and grammar had to replace potentially more complex phrasing. Concrete verbs and nouns took centre stage, doing without the less essential colour of adjectives and adverbs. Imprecision in tenses was accepted; errors were more frequent and more readily ignored. Communication was stripped back to its essence: what happened; where; to whom? "How" was a less frequent question and a flower-strewn "why", perfumed with poetry, was rarely called for.

Perhaps most importantly, Globish cannot draw on the history and idioms of any one culture. All language is ultimately storytelling, and stories require common idioms and shared ideas. We only listen to "Red Riding Hood" because we too are frightened of the wolf in the woods. But Globish has no acknowledged stock of such idioms. The phrase "The Queen's English", for example, is meaningless to people who have no queen and don't know that she might talk in a particular way. The baseball and football references so loved by North American speakers fall flat in a Globish gathering. References to historic events may or may not be understood; references to recent, global news stand a much better chance. The communicator is forced to look deeper, beyond cultural idiom, to find core and universal human truths.

Which is how I made the most astounding discovery of all: the discovery that changed everything about my expectations of church and mission. I discovered that *underneath* our different languages there is a common tongue: the language of humanity. Those who have neither woods nor wolves in their cultural library do, it turns out, have fears. There are common, shared, foundational human experiences that underpin all cultures and unite rather than divide us. There is a central human story. Childbirth and ambition; love and jealousy; sickness, fear and death all belong to this core story. They may find expression in many different language forms, but their presence is universal: they are the basis of what it means to be human.

So the question I learned to ask myself was not so much, "Do you speak Globish?" as "Do you speak Human?" The more I learned to speak Human, the more fully I found myself understood in Globish culture. I found out that the Bible is written in Human. The gospel was made for a Human-speaking world. The importance of this discovery in my own faith journey is huge. It has pressed me to look deeper into the narratives of Scripture and travel further in the fields of culture than ever before. But I would never have made the discovery in the first place if I had not worshipped with the people of forty nations. If I had never been given the challenge of relating faith to diversity, I don't think I would have found the richness of the language of humanity. We used a common language to communicate with one another, but the miracle we shared was that the same God could commune with each of us in our own heart language. God speaks Human – and Human finds its way into meanings that each of us can grasp.

The goal of the New Testament church was not a saved Jewish nation but a redeemed human family. Cultural reconciliation and the cohabitation of diverse and potentially divided people groups was the lifeblood of the new Christian community. When Paul speaks of Jews and Gentiles coming together, the word "Gentile" does not refer to another defined ethnic group. It means "everybody else". Once the Christians had leapt over the big wall separating the Jews from those around them, the implication was that no other wall would stop them. Once you get beyond Judea and Samaria, the ends of the earth become inevitable.

So the first Christian communities began to dream of a

world in which people of every tribe and tongue and language came together. This is the dream we have been grafted into. This is the aspect of the New Testament church without which neither you nor I would ever have been asked to join. No one is suggesting that it was easy, or always successful. There is evidence in the book of Acts that leaping that first wall was a huge challenge, one that took the church not months but years to fully grasp. Some of the lowest moments in the lives and relationships of the apostles came through conflicts over these questions.

But the key is not to examine the success or failure of the apostles so much as to examine their commitment. Hard or easy, fast or slow, they committed themselves to becoming a multi-ethnic church. Diversity is arguably a defining characteristic of the New Testament church. Would we accept it today as a measure of orthodoxy?

For the New Testament Christians the visible manifestation of disparate groups brought together in Christ was the most potent proof that grace worked. Whenever Paul, for example, needed something to point to, to show what grace was for, he would point to reconciliation. To the religious and racial reconciliation of Jews and Gentiles he added that of men and women; of slaves and slave-owners;[6] of educated and uneducated people.[7] The picture is of a community in which groups who had formerly been divided, and were not used to being united, came together.

How will the world be brought together?

Not by the imposition of a single man-made story, but by a larger, God-uttered narrative in which every human story finds its place. God's narrative "translates" into each culture and ultimately into every separate life. We each live in dialogue between God's story and our own. The great thing about the people God has made is this: we are all different enough to be interesting, but similar enough to connect. At heart, we are all made of the same stuff. Human experiences unite us, human concerns are common to us.

And yet we are each unique. Knowing another person, when knowledge runs deeper than "Hello" on the station platform or "Is this seat taken?" adds to my total understanding of the world. Discovering the lives of others; hearing their perspectives; exploring my own assumptions through the lens of theirs: all these are enriching, empowering experiences.

This is why diversity is so important to God's idea of church. The church is an environment in which tribes in tension find the power to coexist. In this redeemed community historic enemies become fellow-travellers. But this is a salad bowl, not a melting pot. The tribes are not homogenized into a bland mush, like Playdough colours mixed once too often. Rather, they are woven together into a beautiful picture – the image of God rediscovered in the colours of the human family. In this unity identity is retained: it is the unity of the collage, not the crowd. And the New Testament attributes this picture not only to a virtual notion of the universal church, but also to an actual vision of the local church: real people in real places displaying the wonder of unity-in-diversity. All cultures. All ages. All classes. All types. Genders and generations together. Each individual finding identity and thriving in community: this is the Bible's description of God's metanational movement. The localized *ekklesia* is a deposit, in each town and city, of God's new and wondrous family.

What changes might your local church need to journey from bland monochrome to glorious colour? Can the Christian church, more than once an active partner in colonial and imperial projects, become again the radically reconciled community our global culture so needs to see?

Think About it: Crowd sourcing

In a talk given for TED Talks[8] in March 2010, Tim Berners-Lee, known as the father of the web,[9] offered a powerful insight into the impact of "crowd sourcing" on web applications. Crowd sourcing turns authority inside out, decentralizing the source of truth and recognizing the wide dispersal of gifting. Crowd sourcing is what happens when all the voices are heard. Information arrived at in this way takes account of the input of "the crowd" rather than that of "the expert". In biblical terms, a commitment to crowd sourcing would arise from the view that God speaks through all his people. The New Testament has its own word for this phenomenon. It is called *Pentecost*.

Task #7: Integration

If we are to follow the New Testament pattern of church – if we aspire to fulfilling God's dream – then we cannot avoid the question of integration. Where sin and conflict have fragmented the human family, redemption integrates. It brings people together, their shared worship flowing from the bedrock of their common humanity to the beauty of their common Redeemer. There is one Creator of all; one Saviour; one baptism by which the followers of Christ are drawn into his one church.

The call of integration will look different in different communities and neighbourhoods, and in different nations. But of this we can be sure: for every local church and for every national church there will be something that needs doing to push the cause of integration forward. Race, gender and social status, among other factors, have been used to segment the human family. We function in sections, and for the most part only know well the people in our own. But the church is a cross-section. Grace cuts across social boundaries. How do we go about the task of integration? Who is God calling us to stand in solidarity with? How can we express our love and appreciation of every shade of humanity? Can we love even those different from us?

What might it mean for your local church to take seriously the task of integration?

The Church You Already Belong to

To embrace Christ is to embrace his desire for one global family. To declare myself a Christian is to step into the most ethnically and culturally diverse movement in history. To name the church the Bride of Christ is to look forward with expectation and joy to a future in which I will stand with the peoples of every tribe and language and, with them, worship the one Lamb. To worship now is to anticipate that future.[1]

Key Text: Romans 15:5–6

May God, who gives this patience and encouragement, help you live in complete harmony with each other, as is fitting for followers of Christ Jesus. Then all of you can join together with one voice, giving praise and glory to God, the Father of our Lord Jesus Christ.[2]

Abstract

Even local churches are called to reflect the global picture of God's family. We are part, already, of a planet-wide people, and the things we do in our own community will either censor or celebrate the beauty of this great treasure.

There are a number of reasons why local churches should aspire to reflect the full colour and diversity of the human family. Two of these are situational: the church already *is* history's most diverse and inclusive religious movement, and the setting in which we serve is also now a rich and diverse ethnic tapestry.

If your local church is a shop window demonstrating the achievements and fruits of grace, then it must, in some sense, declare the wonders of the global church. The seed of the

Christian gospel has been planted into culture after culture, and in every place churches have grown as a result. There is not a single person in your neighbourhood or circle of influence who cannot find their ethnicity mirrored somewhere in the world church. That they don't find it mirrored in yours is a failure not of God's movement but of our capacity to celebrate it.

Timothy Tennent describes the Christian church as "the largest, most ethnically diverse religion in the world" and notes that throughout the twentieth century "a net average gain of 16,500 people were coming to Christ every day in Africa. From 1970 to 1985, for example, the church in Africa grew by over six million people. During that same time, 4,300 people per day were leaving the church in Europe and North America."[3] The church is growing massively in areas we once thought of as "the mission field". The marvellous and many-coloured collage that God is making is already taking shape across the world. Your congregation already is a local branch of a global movement. What can you do to reflect and celebrate this?

As changes have taken place on the world stage, reframing Christianity from being a European export to being a truly global faith, changes have also swept through our "home turf". The contextualizing of the gospel in twenty-first-century culture requires an embracing of diversity. In some cases this calls for a consideration of the immediate neighbourhood a local church serves. If your setting is multi-ethnic but your church is mono-cultural, what can you do? What new prayers can you pray to ask God to paint the wonders of the human family with you? How can the life of your church become "distinctly welcoming"? Should you examine the languages you use; the musical styles you worship in; the ways your church communicates? Are there issues and concerns among the people groups around you that your church can champion? How can you love and serve *all* your neighbours?

In other settings there is a strong case for looking city-wide.

If you are a neighbourhood church and the neighbourhood you work in is monocultural, are there others you can twin with across town, to demonstrate to all the grace and solidarity of Christ? Can you help your neighbours, huddled as they are in the false security of monocultural community, to escape their own captivity and meet the world? What global partnerships can you forge so that the life of your church, week by week, is favoured by the family of God? It may take some time to free your church of the limitations of its single-culture vision, but the starting-point is to say, together and often, "This is not normal." Normative New Testament Christianity includes ethnic reconciliation. Unity in diversity is what grace brings.

Race is only one of the divisions that the church family seeks to overcome, even if it is the most evident. There are also issues around gender, and the way a church celebrates the gifts and contributions all its members bring. And there is age. In a culture in which the needs of marketing have created false distinctions, placing people into age-specific target groups and accentuating the divisions that life-stages can bring, the church can model something different. The cavernous gap between "youth culture" and our fast-growing and long-living population of pensioners is a scandal in our culture.

But does the church seek to bridge this gap, or to reinforce its depths? There is evidence that the best efforts of contextualization by which people are won to the faith – efforts like youth congregations and old people's gatherings – will ultimately prove fruitless unless those reached by them are introduced into the all-age, every-status, multi-ethnic, any-shape-is-a-shape-we-love family of God. We don't of necessity have to spend all our time with people who are not like us. There is scope for age-specific, gender-specific, lifestyle-specific and even race-specific groups to meet and support one another in a church setting. But this is unhealthy unless the wider context also exists and has practical expression. Especially in our public worship, there is a biblical imperative urging us to celebrate diversity.

The development, in the business world, of metanational thinking provides a good model for the kind of communal life we are looking for.[4] A metanational organization, in the minds of those developing such strategies, goes beyond the simple fact of being global or multicultural in make-up. It is not about how many groups constitute the whole, but about what you do with their input. A metanational church would be one that hears from and engages with all the different groups and cultures. It would be a church whose worship life reflects diversity; whose leadership reflects diversity; whose public ministry has the colour and texture that only difference can bring. In the congregational setting, this will mean not just tolerating others, but listening to them; not just acknowledging their existence but celebrating their stories. It means meals together, and conversations. It means friendships that cross ethnic and social boundaries. In the global setting it may mean crossing cultures; seeking opportunities to embrace and know the "other". It may mean championing the cause of a tribe or people group whose plight is all but unknown to your neighbours: singing the song of invisible peoples.

When the musician Gordon Sumner, known the world over as Sting, wanted to champion the cause of the peoples of the Amazon rainforest, he travelled to Brazil to meet with campaigners and activists. He was involved, behind the scenes, in a number of important initiatives. But it was a simple decision that in the end made his campaigning count. He invited activist Raoni Metuktire, a member of an obscure and exotic Amazon tribe, to travel with him. The two appeared on stage together and gave joint interviews on TV shows around the world.

The impact was instant. Metuktire's distinctive appearance, standing beside the very white, very Western Sting, created an iconic image that newspapers loved and audiences talked about.

In the simple act of standing shoulder to shoulder, they put the issues around deforestation onto the agenda of thousands of people who might otherwise not have given them a thought. Some accused Sting of being trite and shallow and said that such an act was mere symbolism. But symbols change lives, and Sting's decision affected people's behaviour. At the very least, he made visible a tribe previously unknown to many in the West.

What can you do to make your church a window into the colour and wonder of God's planet-wide people? We are part of something. It is bigger than our local congregation; bigger than our town; bigger even than our nation and continent. How will we reflect and participate in that panoramic, kaleidoscopic reality?

Think About It: Jesus and the tea ceremony

Though globalization is a phenomenon much accelerated in recent years, it is not entirely new. Cultures have crossed before. Artist Makoto Fujimura recounts a little-known example, when the egalitarian nature of the Christian Eucharist crossed over into one of the world's most ancient civilizations:

> *Sen no Rikyu, the sixteenth-century tea master who is most responsible for the development of the art of tea, lived and died at Daitoku-ji Temple in Kyoto. His tea house still stands there. In China, tea was a form of celebration during banquets, but in Japan, Sen no Rikyu and others refined tea as a form of communication, and the tea house as a minimalist conceptual space. In a war-torn period of cultural flux, Daitoku-ji became the centre of activity, and Sen no Rikyu became a new culture's main voice...*
>
> *His teahouse had a distinctive entry called* nijiri- *guchi, built so small that a guest would have to bow*

and take off his sword in order to pass through it. It is no coincidence (but a historic fact ignored by most in Japan) that one of Rikyu's closest confidantes, one of his wives, was one of the first converts to Christianity under the efforts of Francis Xavier and others, the fruit of an influx of missionaries into Japan in the fifteenth and sixteenth centuries. Rikyu went with his wife to observe a Mass in Kyoto and there saw the Eucharist celebrated with a cup – Christ's blood – being passed around. This experience affirmed his vision for tea. His tea would be an art form: a form of communication equalizing any who took part, shogun or farmer, male or female. Five of Rikyu's seven closest disciples were Christians, later exiled by Shogun Hideyoshi, who gave power and prestige to Sen no Rikyu but later hardened his heart... Hideyoshi realized, quite correctly, that the egalitarian nature of tea would be dangerous to his power, and he became, by no coincidence, one of the greatest enemies of Christianity in history, ordering the execution of thousands of believers and closing Japan to foreigners for several centuries.[5]

This remarkable and little-known story demonstrates the power of the Christian story. Even cultures we think bear no trace of Christian influence may be shaped, in part, by exposure to Christ. Are there traces of the culture of Christ in the lives around you who you think of as not Christian? Is Jesus anonymously hidden in the art and culture that surrounds you?

The Future that Already Holds You

In its eschatological vision of the people of God, looking to the far-future, the New Testament anticipates and proclaims a truly global faith. The followers of Jesus of Nazareth will be drawn from every culture, people-group and language on the face of the earth.[1]

Key Text: Revelation 7:9–10

After this I saw a vast crowd, too great to count, from every nation and tribe and people and language, standing in front of the throne and before the Lamb. They were clothed in white robes and held palm branches in their hands. And they were shouting with a mighty shout, "Salvation comes from our God who sits on the throne and from the Lamb!"[2]

Abstract

The New Testament closes with a vision of God's future church, and sees a multi-ethnic, multilingual global celebration. How does our worship today point towards this future? What does it mean to anticipate the reconciled family of God?

The New Testament church began in a relatively mono-cultural setting. All the first Christians were Jewish. Even moving beyond this to the pro-Jewish Gentiles known as "God-fearers" was a huge step – a paradigm shift described twice in Acts 10 and 11 and widely referred to as "the Gentile Pentecost". But as we have seen, once this first great wall was crossed, others soon followed, and before long Paul, in particular, was preaching to pagans completely outside the influence of Judaism. Many came to faith, and by the time the canon of the New Testament was closed, the faith had spread to a wide diversity of cultures and language groups, and the reality of a community that brought Jews and Gentiles together was established.

But there is more. The New Testament closes not with a celebration of what has happened, but with a glorious vision of what is to come. John's heavenly visions in his Revelation serve a dual purpose for the early church, beginning even then to experience persecution and pressure. Firstly, they seek to pull back the veil that separates earth and heaven, giving insight into the heavenly realities that lie behind earthly experience. John writes to his friends in the churches of Asia Minor to encourage them. Inspired by his prayerful visions, he wants them to know that behind the scenes of their sufferings God is working out his plans. But there is a second veil that John pulls back – the curtain separating the present from the future. Not only is God at work behind the scenes of present-day reality, he is also bringing into being a future, towards which his church is moving. And through visions of this future, John makes an extraordinary claim. He suggests that the faith that has begun to grow beyond its Jewish roots and is spreading into the gardens of neighbouring, pagan nations, will not stop moving until it has touched the very ends of the earth. By the time God's promised future is delivered, people from every tribe and tongue and nation will be engaged in the worship of the Lamb.

John does not see only the tribes and people-groups he already knows are involved. He sees a crowd so vast and diverse that he can only describe it as "every possible flavour". He sees faces he has never seen in the flesh. He hears languages he has never spoken and will never learn. He anticipates a global movement of mission that in reality will wait centuries to be initiated. Worship, John declares, will be displayed in the colours of every human culture. This remarkable vision re-ignited the church of John's day, and has fuelled ever since a passionate belief that Christ is available to all.

And since we believe as churches that our worship, whether in the Eucharist, in song or in our liturgies and readings, is an anticipation of God's promised future, then surely in our worship we should look for these colours? If the very act of worship is an act of eschatological hope, surely it should carry something of John's planet-wide vision? If the church is, as Jurgen Moltmann claims, "an arrow sent into the world to point to its future"[3], what should our public life of worship look like? Can it, even today, reflect the reality of "many languages but only one Lamb"? Can the life of our churches anticipate this coming celebration? If it does not, how will the people of every tribe and culture know that they have been invited to a party?

As the 2012 Spring Harvest Theme Guide says, John's vision of the heavenly future

> is explicitly global in scope and remarkable for its boldness and its breadth: Every tribe and language is included. There will be one family. One body. One bride of Christ – beautiful precisely because she is so colourful. When the focus of the vision shifts and it is a city that John sees, radiant with the splendour of God, he still understands that it will be home to "the nations of the world". The splendour of kings will be brought into this city[4] – the glory and honour of the nations.[5] Despite the limitations of his own experience, John knows that the gospel will go global, and that God is calling to himself one people drawn from the world's many peoples.[6]

Theologians suggest to us that the church now lives as an anticipation of this coming reality: that we are an eschatological people, embodying the hope that the human family can be united; that unity and renewal are possible. You don't have to spend too much time in the major cities of Europe, let alone further afield, to know how desperately such a hope is needed.

Everywhere on earth human beings struggle to embrace the one who is "other", the one who does not belong to my tribe; who does not speak my language. Billions are spent and lost every year in starting and then trying to end the wars that result from our failures in this struggle. Millions have died and are dying still from the simple truth that we do not get on. Can the church anticipate a different future; a kingdom of *shalom*, centred on the Prince of Peace? "The lion will lie down with the lamb," Woody Allen said, "but the lamb won't get much sleep." Can the church prove him wrong? Can we demonstrate today that fear of our fellow human beings is unfounded?

What hope is there for a divided world if the church cannot display the blessings of unity? The call to celebrate diversity is not a duty or a task hovering somewhere near the bottom of the church's list of priorities. It is a joy and privilege, and a central pledge of God's kingdom manifesto.

Think About It: The sad demise of the 50ft Woman

Yvette Vickers, the actress and *Playboy* model whose image was used in the iconic poster for the 1950s film *Attack of the 50ft Woman*, was found dead at her home in May 2011. Though neighbours insisted she still had friends and received correspondence from all over the world, police believe that the eighty-two-year-old may have been dead for up to a year. She was only found there because passers-by noticed that letters stuffed in her post-box were going yellow and that cobwebs had formed at the unopened doorway. Vickers was rumoured to have had affairs with both Lee Marvin and Cary Grant in the 1960s, and appeared briefly alongside Paul Newman in *Hud*. Yet she still died alone, and lay unnoticed for a full year, her body becoming naturally mummified. All this in Beverly Hills, perhaps the world's most prestigious address. If ever there was a measure of the shallowness of celebrity culture and the loss of community in our post-modern world, this is it. If we measured success and afforded fame in terms not of money and adulation, but of relational wealth, our world would be a more comforting place by far.

What challenges does an incident like this present for the people of God? How many others are there in our communities who are not part of any family or group that will notice their absence over a twelve-month period? Can the church build the kind of community in which this does not happen?

Gauguin's Angel

God is the ultimate polyglot, speaking every language known and inviting every human being to pray in their own mother tongue. How can a church resulting from the love of such a God not be globally diverse?[1]

Key Text: Mark 16:20

And the disciples went everywhere and preached, and the Lord worked through them, confirming what they said by many miraculous signs.[2]

Abstract

Part of the church's task is to bring the story of God alive in ever new cultural settings. As we translate God's story into the lives and languages of those around us, what dreams and visions do we inspire in them? Who is waiting for you to be the translator, for them, of God's story?

Central to the church's journey to God's multilingual future is the principle of translation. Translation makes the spread of faith possible. The Christian story finds a home in every human culture it encounters. It rests there, settling in, shedding light on local sights and customs, until in time it begins its deep, organic work of transformation. It is central to the story of the church that we engage in the constant, forward-moving translation of the story of God into ever new cultures and people groups.

This is not simply a question of the actual translation of words from one language to another – though that in itself is a great adventure, and a glittering part of the whole pageant. Rather, the missional translation of God's story is the arrival of Christ in each new cultural group. It is Jesus moving into the

neighbourhood; Jesus making himself known and understood in the heart-dialect of those receiving him.

Paul Gauguin is honoured as one of the greatest artists in history. His place as a vital link in the chain that led from Impressionism to the art of the twentieth century is acknowledged, and he bequeathed to the world some of the most beautiful works of his generation. Among these is a canvas painted in Brittany in 1888, not long before Gauguin left France for self-imposed exile in Tahiti. Technically, the painting is noted for its use of a bold, strong red to establish the field within which its story is told.[3]

But the story itself is also unique. In the foreground of the picture a group of Breton peasant women gather. Dressed in their Sunday best, their black dresses and white headpieces dominate the bottom half of the canvas. They crowd together to look at a field, in which two things are happening, divided by the branch of a tree that Gauguin uses to designate two different spheres of action. On one side an ordinary Breton calf grazes, much as Breton calves are prone to do on any given day of the week. On the other side, though, something more dramatic is happening. An angel, man-sized but glorious in the spread of his golden wings, is wrestling with a man, bent double in his simple black robe. In the frozen moment of time that the picture captures, the angel appears to be winning.

As is often the case with Gauguin, it is the title of the picture that gives it its true drama – and makes it meaningful even today. It is called *Vision After the Sermon*. Gauguin was not himself a man of faith, but he was fascinated by the faith of others. In particular, he was drawn to the childlike faith of simple, peasant communities. When he later moved to Tahiti, he became deeply, almost obsessively interested in the primitive, pagan beliefs of the simple tribespeople he met there. But even before this, in France, he saw the same power to believe in the people of Brittany. The women he depicts in *Vision After the*

Sermon are on their way home from church. But so arresting has the sermon they have listened to been; so dramatic its portrayal of Jacob's angelic encounter; so gripping its narrative, that it is as if, walking home, they see Jacob there, in their own field, wrestling still.

Gauguin uses the technique of the divided canvas, with the calf on the other side of the tree, to make a statement. The plane of the vision has come to rest alongside the plane of reality. They share the same red ground. The dream has landed here, in this field, in this peasant Breton community. It is in their reality that the women meet Jacob, and watch him fight his angel.

For a man whose own faith was eclectic and confused, as informed by the paganism of Polynesia as by the Catholicism of his upbringing, Gauguin had a remarkable handle on the meaning of Christian mission. He captured for all time the idea of the Bible becoming vivid in the life of those who hear it – as real to them in their culture as it was to its original protagonists in theirs. This angel touches the lives of these women with no less real a touch than that with which he first visited Jacob. Faith has landed. It has been earthed. God's story is real in their field.

Who is there, in your community or circle of influence, who is waiting for you to translate the story of God? The true hero of Gauguin's painting is neither shown nor named. Even as the women see their vision, there is a simple Catholic priest, somewhere too far away to be featured in the picture. He is walking home to his own table, perhaps questioning whether anything he has said has had meaning for his congregation. Asking if it is worth it, this week-by-week effort to bring God's story alive. Wondering if anyone is listening. A simple priest, whose handling of Scripture, unknown to him, has set a fire in the imaginations of his people.

The texts of Scripture address each and every human culture. Christianity is uniquely marked, in the words of the missiologist Andrew Walls, by the "Translation Principle".[4] The translatability of Scripture has brought the faith into ever new cultural fields, continually sparking "interactions with new areas of thought and custom".[5] This expansion through translation is rooted in the very origins of Christian belief, where the incarnation, "the translation of the word into flesh",[6] forms the very basis of our faith, and continues to carry the gospel into new cultures today.

When the Bible "arrives" in a new culture, it is speaking a language that the Creator already knows, to hearts the Creator dreamed of, designed, fashioned and has loved from the founding of the world. Even if the result is for us a "new" translation, it is no such thing to its author. Scripture addresses fundamental human concerns; issues common to all created beings. The texts of Scripture throw light on the horizon of the world into which they were first written, but they lend their light also to the horizons of subsequent and different worlds, and they throw light forward into ours. Both the actual translation of biblical texts into new languages and the cultural translation of the church into new settings are expressions of the central, incarnational thrust of the gospel. There is no world so distant or so strange that God's word cannot be earthed in it, and no human being alive whose heart is not potentially God's home.

Task #8: Translation

Andrew Walls asserts the place of translation in the global church, and has explored this predominantly in the context of world mission. But as Lesslie Newbigin, Alan Roxburgh, Al Hirsch and others have shown, this vital task is also urgent for the local church. Even in our own neighbourhood, we can no longer assume that people speak the language of the church. In many senses we continue to express our faith in words and codes developed for an age long since ended. Our in-church language bears little relation to the languages of the culture around us. This can be a pressing issue for a local church, since so much of what we do is about rituals and stories that come, by definition, from the past. We come together around the repetition of key ideas and formulations. We use liturgies and songs that are familiar precisely because we have used them before. The unity we experience within the church is reinforced by these rituals and repetitions.

But we cannot ignore the call to translate. We must balance our need for familiarity with our need to be understood. Translation doesn't dilute our message – it makes it stronger. Every new culture added to the family of God brings with it jewels of humanity. We get richer as we cross cultural boundaries.

What people groups are there in your surroundings who need to hear the story of God translated? What can you do to move towards them? What acts of translation is God calling you to?

After Athens

All too often we fail to listen because we have assumed that our own culture is normative, and that others should adapt to us. The gospel, by contrast, challenges us to do the adapting.[1]

Key Text: Acts 17:25–26

He himself gives life and breath to everything, and he satisfies every need. From one man he created all the nations throughout the whole earth. He decided beforehand when they should rise and fall, and he determined their boundaries.[2]

Abstract

Just as Jesus is the Jewish Messiah, fulfilling every hope and promise of Israel's history, so he completes every human culture. There is no human culture to which Christ's story does not bring fulfilment and hope.

For many missionaries and Bible translators, confidence in the capacity of God's story to earth itself in new cultural settings is inspired by a story contained in the Bible itself. Paul's visit to Athens, when a glitch in travel plans left him stranded for several days, became a watershed encounter for the Christian missionary movement.

Paul is at first shocked – the sense of the Greek is "sickened" – by the idolatry of Athens. To a Jewish scholar educated among the Pharisees, idolatry is a kind of pornography: it is a practice a rabbi doesn't want to be seen even near to. Paul's Jewish roots urge him to flee from idolatry; to put some miles, or at the very least some walls, between himself and these idols. But the Holy Spirit has other ideas, and Paul is led to look more closely. He begins to examine the many idols of Athens, and a new truth dawns on him. At the heart of this idolatry is a human search for God. The objects of worship may be false, but the motivation is real. The people of Athens are reaching for a God they do not know but suspect might be there. And Paul knows his name.

Paul connects with the search of these people. Far from condemning their idolatry, he sees it as step one in a journey that will ultimately bring them to Christ. And then he does something that has never been done before. He gives away the Jewish story. Paul is the first to fully understand that a faith community could be faithful to Jewish history without being Jewish. It can do so because God is the Creator of all: salvation is not a Jewish story but a human one. Paul "humanizes" the Jewish narrative. Where the Jews have for centuries thought of themselves as a God-forged nation, born of one man, Abraham, and given the land of promise, Paul goes further back, to Adam, and declares that we are all such nations:

> The God who made the world and everything in it is the
> Lord of heaven and earth and does not live in temples
> built by human hands. And he is not served by human
> hands, as if he needed anything. Rather, he himself gives
> everyone life and breath and everything else. From one
> man he made all the nations, that they should inhabit the
> whole earth; and he marked out their appointed times in
> history and the boundaries of their lands. God did this so
> that they would seek him and perhaps reach out for him
> and find him, though he is not far from any one of us.
> "For in him we live and move and have our being." As
> some of your own poets have said, "We are his offspring."[3]

Through his deep knowledge of the Jewish faith, Paul has wrestled with the question of continuity. As a Jewish scholar he believes that God is one – that God the Creator is the God

Yahweh active in the exodus and that the God Yahweh has come to us in the Messiah, Jesus. The two gardens – that of Eden and that of the resurrection – are the playgrounds of the same Holy Spirit. Jesus the Messiah fulfils the redemptive promise of Israel. He is the answer to every question raised by Israel's history. He is the fulfilment of every hope. Israel's story, looking as it does to God's future and longing as it does for God's Messiah, finds completion in Christ.

Paul has spoken face to face with hundreds of Jews, and has told each one of them: "Jesus completes the Jewish story." But in Athens he faces people who do not live in the Jewish story; who do not even know it. And he discovers, wandering their streets and watching them at worship, a truth that will change his life forever, and touches ours even today: "Jesus completes every human story." You don't have to live in the Jewish story before you can embrace the story of Christ, because Christ is the Messiah for every human story. He is the answer to every question raised by your history. He is the fulfilment of your every hope. Your story, looking as it does, even unknowingly, to God's future, and longing as it does, even unknowingly, for God's Messiah, can find completion in Christ.

As he engaged in dialogue with believers from non-Jewish cultures, strangers to the narratives of Genesis and Exodus; to the rites and rituals of the Jerusalem Temple; to the rich history of kings and prophets, Paul's concern was that they should be free to improvise their own place in God's story while being faithful to the witness of history. He was himself deeply rooted in the Jewish narrative but he sought to aid non-Jewish communities as they worked out what their own story should be. Every nation, he discovered, can find the key to its redemptive history in Christ.

Every act of Bible translation that there has ever been, every step in cross-cultural mission, is authorized by Paul's discovery in Athens. After Athens, every human culture becomes open to the earthing of Christ in its history. It is only a matter of time before people from every tribe and tongue and nation will discover that the God they worship without knowing has a name.

Do you believe that among the people you work with and converse with each day; among those who surround the building or buildings you use as a church to gather in; among those you have contact with or influence over, or simply hang out with on Facebook, are those who worship God without knowing? Do you know people whose loves and longings, written in the language of humanity, are the same loves and longings that, in your life, lead to worship?

Think About It: Dear Lulu

At Easter 2011, a letter was published that was written by the Archbishop of Canterbury, Rowan Williams, in response to one he had received from Lulu, a six-year-old Scottish girl. Lulu's letter was addressed to God, and said, "To God, How did you get invented?" Her father, who is not a believer, sent her letter to various church leaders. Some of the replies he received were complex and theological. That from Dr Williams was noted for its simplicity and clarity. He wrote:

> *Dear Lulu,*
> *Your dad has sent on your letter and asked if I have any answers. It's a difficult one! But I think God might reply a bit like this –*
> *"Dear Lulu – Nobody invented me – but lots of people discovered me and were quite surprised. They discovered me when they looked round at the world and thought it was really beautiful or really mysterious and wondered where it came from. They discovered me when they were very very quiet on their own and felt a sort of*

*peace and love they hadn't expected. Then they invented
ideas about me – some of them sensible and some of
them not very sensible. From time to time I sent them
some hints – specially in the life of Jesus – to help them
get closer to what I'm really like. But there was nothing
and nobody around before me to invent me. Rather like
somebody who writes a story in a book, I started making
up the story of the world and eventually invented human
beings like you who could ask me awkward questions!"*

*And then he'd send you lots of love and sign off. I
know he doesn't usually write letters, so I have to do the
best I can on his behalf. Lots of love from me too.*

+Archbishop Rowan

How does the Archbishop's letter read in the light of Paul's
sermon to the philosophers of Athens? How does it value and
validate the spiritual searches human beings engage in? How
might Lulu feel, fifteen years from now, when she reads the
letter again on her twenty-first birthday?

Epilogue
The Most Brilliant Idea Ever

I See A New City

In the New Testament context the church is the community through whom God is now working to bless the nations of the earth. Theirs is not a passive or static calling but a dynamic invitation to co-operate with God in the healing of creation: to engage with the Trinity in a life-wide dance as purposeful as it is beautiful.[1]

Key Text: Matthew 6:10

May your Kingdom come soon.
May your will be done on earth,
as it is in heaven.[2]

Abstract

The polarity of our story is a move from heaven to earth. The city God is building will be rooted in our soil. The church lives now in the light of this future. We dream God's dream. Will we rise up and build?

Burt Lancaster. Montgomery Clift. Deborah Kerr. Frank Sinatra. When *From Here to Eternity* hit cinema screens in 1953 it was hailed as "The boldest book of our time – honestly, fearlessly on the screen." Controversial in its day; passionate; dramatic, the film created iconic scenes that became part of movie history. And its title slipped into the English language, giving pastors and preachers an open goal to score in. Because, after all, isn't that exactly what our bold book is about – the journey of humanity from here to eternity?

Except that it isn't, and that one error has done more damage to the life of the church than any other in our history. If the story of the Bible were expressed in a film title, it wouldn't

173

be *From Here to Eternity*. It would be *From Eternity to Here*. The Bible does not describe the movement of people from earth to heaven – it tells the story of the flow of God's blessings from heaven to earth. The prayer Jesus taught us to pray, in simple words that were to be our daily food and water, the bread and butter of our faith, was a prayer for God's will to be done *here*, for his kingdom to come on *earth*. It is a prayer that moves from there to here; from God's world into ours; from the courts of heaven to the soil of earth.

How we could have re-engineered such a magnificent story to present it as a rescue plan for disembodied souls is mind-boggling, but that is what we have done. Even the pearly gates, our favourite image of heaven – familiar to millions and reproduced in jokes, cartoons and birthday cards the world over – are not what they seem. They are not, in John's vision, cloud-bound and set at the entrance of heaven. They are, rather, set at the twelve entrances to the City of God – and they are anchored in the soil of earth.[3] John's vision of the future contains an unambiguous polarity. The City of God comes "down from God out of heaven"[4] and the final great cry of triumph is not "now people can live with God" but "Look, God's home is now among his people! He will live with them, and they will be his people. God himself will be with them."[5]

Centuries before this moment, in a garden still west with dew, God came looking for a man and woman he had made. They were hiding from him, ashamed of what they had done. But why was he looking for them? What was his purpose? It was to walk with them in the garden in the cool of the evening.[6] God did not make the earth to be their home alone. He made it to be his, with them. This is the Bible's polarity, established in its very first pages and reaffirmed in its last: it is the direction of the movement of the purposes of God. It underpins everything. The gospel is a one-way street running from heaven to earth.

There is a temptation to suggest that such things mean little to the life of the church in the everyday. How can such esoteric claims, drawn from the legends of the deep past and expressed in dreams of the far future, make a difference to us now? But they make all the difference in the world. To misconstrue the polarity of the gospel is to fundamentally misunderstand its purpose. What message will we give to our neighbours; what gospel will we preach; what stories will we tell, if we are reading the whole of God's drama *backwards*? Might this be the source of our lifelessness, the reason for our loss of colour? Is the dull greyness of our church experience the fruit of trying to run up the down escalator: loading heaven-bound lifeboats while the angels are filling earth-bound supply ships?

Leonard Sweet has suggested that we are in the midst of "a new kind of war – a 'Story War'". The winner, he says, is "the one who narrates the best story".[7] To believers more used to defending their truths than their stories, this may seem a little too loose and casual. Stories, after all, are notoriously difficult to pin down in terms of propositions. But propositions, on the other hand, are notoriously difficult to pass on or live with beyond a generation or so. The world changes daily. Language evolves. Meanings shift. It is precisely by not being precise that stories survive. Story speaks to the truths that propositions would only imprison. Sometimes the best way to preserve a timeless truth is to hide it in a story. What story do we have for our world at the bedtime of its years?

Sweet is referring, I think, to the cultural battle between the Christian story and competing narratives. But this is not the only war we're caught up in. There is also a civil war within the community of faith as we battle over just what story we will tell – about ourselves and about our God. Challenged to summarize the Bible's story, many Christians will say that it is a narrative of two destinations. Everyone goes to heaven or hell. Both are forever and neither are here, and this is what the gospel is all about. But dramatic as this story may be, it isn't the story the Bible tells.

The God who made the world, in all its beautiful, multi-layered, prismatic complexity, and who placed within it human beings gifted with the spark of his life and breath and commissioned to care for it, is the same God who has come to us in poverty, suffered and died and risen in power and is ready now, to fill each one of us with his new life. This God will come to us again to free the whole created order – all that he has made *in all its beautiful, multi-layered, prismatic complexity* – from the bondage of sin. Freedom is coming. It's coming. Listen. The leaves of the trees are rustling. We hear hoofbeats. On the far horizon, a cloud no bigger than the fist of a man is rising. A wind is stirring. A song is rising. The groaning of the earth grows deeper. The moment of new birth is near.

The church of Christ is the beginning of a new song for creation. It is a movement we join *now*, a song we sing *now*, a dream we dream *now* in anticipation of all that is to come. The colours we see swirling in the worship of the church are the colours of sunrise, the first bright shining of a new day waking. We are the Spirit's dawn chorus.

Our model in this journey towards God's city of the future, according to the writer to the Hebrews, is Abraham, the father of our faith and much more besides. We are told of Abraham that "even when he reached the land God promised him, he lived there by faith – for he was like a foreigner, living in tents… Abraham was confidently looking forward to a city with eternal foundations, a city designed and built by God."[8]

By living in a tent Abraham gave birth to a spirit of adventure and exploration that has shaped more than a third of the world's population. Whole cultures have come into being because of one man's courageous camping. Christians are glad to number themselves among the children of Abraham, but tend to interpret the temporary nature of the Patriarch's accommodation as an "earth to heaven" paradigm. A temporary sojourner on earth, Abraham was waiting; anticipating; moving towards the joys of heaven.

But as we have seen, this is the very opposite of the story the Bible has for us. Abraham didn't live under canvas because he was just passing through, on his journey to a home elsewhere. He lived the life of a camper because he was waiting to inherit the campsite. Every tent-peg the old man and his family drove into the ground reminded them that this very soil had been promised to them. They lived in tents *in the land* that God had said would one day be theirs. Abraham is not a model of the kind of faith that waits to be taken to a better place. He is a model of the kind of faith that knows that this place will one day be better.

This switches the polarity of Abraham's engagement with his culture. When he confronts the fact that he is not the current owner of the land he stands on, he doesn't think, "This is tough, but I won't be here for ever." Rather, he looks in the eye of those who do hold the present deeds and says in his heart, or perhaps even mutters under his breath, "This is tough, but *you* won't be here forever." When an Abrahamic faith confronts addiction, child abuse, pornography, violence and poverty, when it looks in the eye all that distorts the image of God in men and women, it doesn't think, "It's tough now, but my days here are numbered." It looks, rather, in the face of evil and says, "It's tough now, but *your* days here are numbered." We are not waiting to escape planet earth, but to inherit it. It is to sin and death and suffering, to tears and crying and pain, that God has issued an eviction notice. What a difference it makes to know that you are not promised rescue but redemption.

What gave Abraham the capacity to wait in this way? To ever believe while never seeing? In a word, God. Abraham believed that his future was in the gift of a being outside himself: a divine person who could be trusted. The promise had not come from a random universe, but from a loving Creator. Abraham and his sons were not waiting in the vain hope that things might one day take a turn for the better. They were not, week on week, buying lottery tickets. It was not fate, or circumstance, or their own ingenuity and effort that would build God's city. The word of promise had come from God himself, who loved them and had spoken to them. You cannot trust history, or destiny, or the market in such a way. Trust is personal: it is person-centred. The key to Abraham's story, so much the foundation of our own, is the I–Thou relationship at its heart: his journey is a spiritual quest. It's not only Abraham's spirit of adventure that our culture needs. We need to trust in Abraham's God.

But there is one last question we should ask of this image of Abraham's tent. Why did he not buy a farm? Clearly he had cash. He had done well for himself. When he looked for a field in which to bury his much-loved Sarah, he was willing to pay. So why did he never buy a farm? Even if he was waiting for God's city, why not settle in the meantime – take what you can get? Why not build a fence and a nice wooden house and live secure within the borders of your own prosperity? The answer is that God had promised him a nation. Abraham faced a daily choice – the certainty of a farm or the promise of a nation. Small and certain blessings now, or unnumbered blessings forged from a future walked in faith with God.

I face the same choice every day, as does every church (and every person) that seeks to follow Christ. A farm now, or a future by faith? A tiny church today, or a world transformed tomorrow? Little rewards for my paltry efforts, or the joy of playing my part in the chain of faith that leads towards much more? Will you settle for the small reward of a fenced-in, wooden-shack church? Or will you dream God's dream, groaning with the Spirit for the freedom of creation? Perhaps Abraham, when the simple certainties of farming tempted him, raised his eyes to the horizon and settled his soul with just two words: "All this." What if we could do the same?

As we have seen already, such a walk into God's future begins in the imagination. In his letter to the Ephesians, Paul appeals to the God who "is able to do immeasurably more than all we ask or imagine, according to his power that is at work within us".[9] As we wrestle to rediscover purpose and colour in our journey with God through human culture; as we look for the next phase of this adventure called church; as we walk with humble determination into the future God has for us, can we too recover Abraham's dream? Can we believe that God will transform his world? Do we see the city he is building? As the Spring Harvest Theme Guide says: "The Holy Spirit is not only forming each of us after the likeness of Christ, but is forming us together, as church, to fulfil God's purposes in our time and context. He is the deposit guaranteeing our inheritance, pointing us towards the plans of God. In each new generation, the voice of the Spirit calls the church onwards to God's future."[10]

The power of the imagination to shape the church has been proved before. It is at the heart of the vision we have already referred to, that of the apostle John, exiled on the island of Patmos. At a time when the first generation of Christ's followers faced enormous pressure – from persecution; from the loss experienced in the death of the original apostles; from the evident delay of Christ's return – the apostle John sought solace in solitude with God. Exiled to a wild and wind-beaten island, he wrestled in prayer for the churches he knew and so loved. The result was the vision recorded in the book of Revelation, containing some of the most powerful and dramatic imagery in all of Scripture. This vision of a future church blending disciples from every tribe and culture culminates in the declaration of God's presence among us, pictured as the coming of the City of God. John's prayers and visions are an extraordinary testament to the power of imagination. Decisively they set the fledgling church on the path to becoming a global, multi-ethnic planet-transforming force. They raised the early Christians' sights beyond the furthest horizon. They gave God's people a dream.

The great apostle hears the words declared from heaven: "Look, I am making everything new!"[11] His vision seems to be of future events, and is set in the context of prophetic imagery drawn from the past, from the proclamations of Daniel, Isaiah and Ezekiel. There are traces of the language of Eden and echoes of the dream of Abraham. Yet the voice speaks in the present tense. Past, present and future merge in a dramatic declaration of the purposes of God. Not only does John's vision give us insight into what God has done and is doing in the world, it also answers the question, "What is God doing right now?" In any given time and setting, John implies, the events we see unfolding before us can be read against two horizons – the horizon of all that God has done and spoken in the past, and the horizon of all he has promised for the future. The purposes of God are like an underground river, flowing invisibly beneath the events of history. Rooted in the world's in-God beginnings and moving towards its promised in-God end, these purposes are always consistent with God's character. The best way to understand the present is to have God's perspective on the past and future. From the "it was very good" of Genesis 1 to the "all things new" of Revelation 21, visible history is a reflection of God's unseen plans, and can only truly be interpreted by their light.

"I see a new city" is a poem written in the light of this dream, recorded on the *Restore* CD and DVD. Inspired by John's vision on the isolated island of Patmos, it asks what vision inspires us. What do we see as we look to the cities of Europe? What future waits for us? Nothing comes into being that is not first imagined. The energy of our participation in the building of God's kingdom will be dictated by the strength of our dreams. If we can't see it as possible, how will we work for it? If it does not live in us as a dream, how will it live through us in reality?

I see a new city

I see a new city, poured out from Heaven
Dressed for a party; blazing with beauty
Her rooftops are radiant, trees trembling with laughter
And joy like a jewel shines in her streets

From her walls and windows
No weeping is heard
Through her gateways and gutters
Floods of tears do not flow
For in her homes and houses no pain dwells
Bricks once broken down in mourning
Rise again in song and celebration
Stones thrown down by enmity and envy
Dare to dance in swirling swathes of mercy

She sings: a million voices rising
The long-lost languages of human hopes
The secret praise of human hearts, released at last
Because her God is with her
Because his home is made
Within her walls
Because his voice is heard
Gentle like the rains of spring
Declaring: New! New! New!
I am making all things New

This is the city I see
The future I belong to
This is the blueprint my heart holds on to
Even now, in streets that sing another story

Even here, beneath a darker vision's shadow
This metropolis of mercy
Promising future realization
Active now in love's imagination
This is my dream
And though I wait, and though I long
And though the sacred city may seem slow:
Still I will hope
Still I will pray
Still I will today
Rise up and build[12]

If this is the dream that inspires us, if this is the vision that invades our imagination, what acts of investment does it call us to today? Vinay Samuel suggested that mission consists of "finding out where God is already at work and who God is using already. This is a reversal from evangelical mission of the past. God is already ahead of me. Who is he working with? Where is the evidence of his work?"[13]

What if God is, by his Spirit, making all things new?

Now?

In the present tense?

In us and around us and in every corner of the world?

What if a new world is coming to birth around us? What if the very ground we pitch our tents on is pregnant with the purposes of God? What should we pray for if this is the case? How should we work? What kinds of communities of faith should we be, if we are to point the world towards its promised future?

Perhaps it is the knowledge of this future; the promise of this renewal; the declaration of this intimate involvement of God in the very atoms of our world, that makes the church "an explosion of joy" in our world. Is this the big picture we've been looking for? Is this the story God was telling, through an empty frame, on a sunlit beach in the fishing village of Collioure?

Notes

Introduction

1. Gerard Kelly, "Consider", *twitturgies*, 4 February 2009, www.twitter.com/twitturgies

2. http://www.collioure.com/gb/dec_gb.htm (accessed 5 Feb. 2010).

3. http://www.collioure.com.au/fauvism.htm (accessed 5 Feb. 2010).

4. http://www.collioure.com.au/matisse4.htm (accessed 5 Feb. 2010).

5. Leonard Sweet, www.twitter.com/lensweet (11 Sept. 2010).

6. Psalm 78:4 NLT.

7. I recommend the work of Stuart Murray in the post-Christendom series, Paternoster, 2004, 2005; Al Hirsch, *The Forgotten Ways*, Brazos Press, 2007; Hirsch and Frost, *The Shaping of Things to Come*, Hendrickson, 2003.

8. James Thwaites, *Church Beyond the Congregation*, Paternoster, 2002, was widely received in this way, even if this was not intended.

9. Gerard Kelly, *Get a Grip on the Future*, Monarch, 1998; published in the USA as *Retrofuture*, IVP, 2000.

Assembly Lines

1. *Church Actually*, the Spring Harvest Theme Guide 2012.

2. Acts 19:32.

3. Deuteronomy 23ff; 1 Chronicles 28:8.

4. Cited in Veli-Matti Kärkkäinen, *An Introduction to Ecclesiology: Ecumenical, Historical and Global Perspectives*, IVP, 2002.

5. Mark Tedder and the Worshiplanet Band, "Restore", Worshiplanet Inc.

6. © Gerard Kelly 2010.

Prismatic People

1. *Church Actually*, the Spring Harvest Theme Guide 2012.

2. Ephesians 3:10.

3. Ephesians 3:10–11.

4. Matthew 5:13–14 The Message.

5. See Isaiah 28:24–29 The Message.

The King's Dome

1. *Church Actually*, the Spring Harvest Theme Guide 2012.

2. Matthew 11:12.

3. Jurgen Moltmann, cited in Veli-Matti Kärkkäinen, *An Introduction to Ecclesiology: Ecumenical, Historical and Global Perspectives*, IVP, 2002.

4. Artist and critic Robert Kushner, cited in *Reflections*, Yale Divinity School, Vol 96, Number 1, Spring 2009.

Mission is a Mirror-Ball

1. *Church Actually*, the Spring Harvest Theme Guide 2012.

2. John 15:5 NLT.

3. Ephesians 4:11–13 NLT.

4. Crossroads International Church, www.xrds.nl where I was Senior Pastor from 2005 to 2009.

5. Abraham Kuyper, cited in Richard Mouw, "MINE! Kuyper for a new century", *Comment Magazine*, 22 June 2007, http://www.cardus.ca/comment/

Human Church

1. Matthew 5:13–14 The Message.

2. *Church Actually*, the Spring Harvest Theme Guide 2012.

3. 1 Peter 1:12 NLT.

4. Job 1:6–12 offers a good representation of a traditional Hebrew cosmology.

5. Al Wolters, *Creation Regained: Biblical Basics for a Reformational Worldview*, Eerdmans, 1985 and 2005.

Fresh from the Factory

1. *Church Actually*, the Spring Harvest Theme Guide 2012.

2. Genesis 1:27–28 NLT.

3. Ephesians 2:10.

4. Ephesians 1:4.

5. 1 Corinthians 2:7.

6. Hans Küng, *The Church*, Continuum, 2001, p. 272, cited in Veli-Matti Kärkkäinen, *An Introduction to Ecclesiology: Ecumenical, Historical and Global Perspectives*, IVP, 2002.

7. "You can't imagine all that God can do with your life."

8. Matthew 5:13–16 NLT.

9. © Gerard Kelly, May 2011.

Your Call is Important to Us

1. *Church Actually*, the Spring Harvest Theme Guide 2012.

2. Ephesians 2:10 NLT.

3. Evelyn and James Whitehead, *Seasons of Strength: New Visions of Adult Christian Maturing*, Doubleday, 1984.

4. Ephesians 4:13 NLT: "This will continue until we all come to such unity in our faith and knowledge of God's Son that we will be mature in the Lord, measuring up to the full and complete standard of Christ."

5. Ephesians 2:10.

6. Ephesians 4:13.

7. Ken Robinson with Lou Aronica, *The Element: How Finding Your Passion Changes Everything*, Viking, 2009.

8. You can watch the advert at http://www.youtube.com/watch?v=IU caM_0ztbM&feature=related

9. Ephesians 4:13.

10. Ephesians 3:20.

11. Dan Davidson, Dave Davidson and George Verwer, *God's Great Ambition*, ThinkWow.com, 2001.

Charismystic Community

1. Gerard Kelly, "Clouds", *twitturgies*, 27 June 2009, www.twitter.com/twitturgies

2. Ephesians 4:4 NLT.

3. www.24-7prayer.com

4. Pete Greig and Andy Freeman, *Punk Monk: New Monasticism and the Ancient Art of Breathing*, Regal, 2007.

5. http://pfaffe3000.typepad.com/blog/

6. See http://www.mateno.org/projekte/bethanien

7. http://www.mateno.org/

8. http://frohmagazin.de/

9. http://www.apostleschurch.org/

10. See http://www.moot.uk.net/about/rhythm-of-life/

11. Rory Fitzpatrick, "Rebels With a Cause", *The Tablet*, 13 March 2010.

12. Fitzpatrick, "Rebels With a Cause".

13. Henri Nouwen, 1997 in *Weavings, A Journal of the Spiritual Life*, Nashville, The Upper Room, 1996-2012, see http://weavings.upperroom.org/

14. Os Guinness, *The Call: Finding and Fulfilling the Central Purpose of Your Life*, Thomas Nelson, 2003.

15. Dallas Willard, *The Spirit of the Disciplines: Understanding How God Changes Lives*, HarperOne, 1990.

16. Charles de Foucault, private letter, 1901, cited in Sara Maitland, *A Book of Silence*, Granta, 2008.

17. Sarah Maitland, *A Book of Silence*.

Discovering Fire

1. *Church Actually*, the Spring Harvest Theme Guide 2012.

2. Acts 2:3 NLT.

3. Dallas Willard, *Renovation of the Heart: Putting on the Character of Christ*, Colorado Springs: NavPress, 2002.

4. Acts 17:25, 28 NLT.

5. Ephesians 4:13 NLT.

6. Simon Ponsonby, *More: How you can have more of the Spirit when you already have everything in Christ*, David C. Cook, 2004.

7. John 6:1–13.

8. John 6:7.

A Gift Economy

1. *Church Actually*, the Spring Harvest Theme Guide 2012.

2. Ephesians 4:8 NLT.

3. Psalm 68:18 NLT.

4. Ephesians 4:8 NLT.

5. John 16:7 NLT.

6. Ephesians 2:10 NLT.

7. Acts 17:25 NLT.

8. Acts 17:28.

9. Ephesians 4:7 NLT.

10. Ephesians 4:11 NLT.

11. Ephesians 4:12 NLT.

Honoured Architects

1. *Church Actually*, the Spring Harvest Theme Guide 2012.

2. John 13:14 NLT.

3. Isaiah 58:10.

4. Mark 2:27.

5. Matthew 13:31–32 NLT.

6. © Gerard Kelly, April 2011, www.blessnet.eu

Transformant Task Force

1. Gerard Kelly, "Continue Us", *twitturgies*, 9 March 2009, www.twitter.com/twitturgies

2. Colossians 1:9–10 NLT.

3. Ephesians 1:3–9.

4. Colossians 1:6, 10.

5. Romans 12:1–2 NLT.

6. IVP, 1995.

7. Gregory A. Boyd, *Seeing Is Believing: Experience Jesus Through Imaginative Prayer*, Baker Books, 2004.

8. See http://www.gregboyd.org/books/seeing-is-believing/

9. See http://www.gregboyd.org/books/seeing-is-believing/

Rooted and Booted

1. *Church Actually*, the Spring Harvest Theme Guide 2012.

2. John 15:5 NLT.

3. Ephesians 3:17 NLT.

4. Ephesians 3:18 NLT.

5. Romans 8:22 NLT.

6. Romans 8:26 NLT.

7. © Gerard Kelly 2010.

Charlie Chaplin's Cane

1. *Church Actually*, the Spring Harvest Theme Guide 2012.
2. Philippians 2:4–5 J. B. Phillips New Testament.
3. Anne Rice, *Christ the Lord: Out of Egypt*, Ballantine Books, 2008.
4. Anne Rice, *Christ the Lord: The Road to Cana*, Ballantine Books, 2009.
5. Anne Rice, *Called Out of Darkness, A Spiritual Confession*, Anchor, 2008.
6. See James 2:5, where James directly identifies the "poor of this world" as those who will "inherit the kingdom".
7. Philippians 2:6–11.
8. Philippians 2:5.

Meekonomics

1. *Church Actually*, the Spring Harvest Theme Guide 2012.
2. Isaiah 11:4 NKJV.
3. Psalm 37:10–11 NLT.
4. Isaiah 11:4 NLT.
5. Gerard Kelly, "Meekonomics", *twitturgies*, 2 April 2009, www.twitter.com/twitturgies
6. David Smith, *Mission After Christendom*, Darton, Longman and Todd, 2003.

Metanational Movement

1. Gerard Kelly, "To Boldly Go", *twitturgies*, 25 June 2009, www.twitter.com/twitturgies
2. Ephesians 2:17–18 NLT.
3. http://www.kickitout.org
4. The advert can be viewed at http://www.youtube.com/watch?v=N14Lbwk7q34&
5. Cited in *Time Magazine*, http://www.time.com/time/magazine/article/0,9171,1950943,00.html#ixzz1b2WfDX7Y
6. Galatians 3:28.
7. Colossians 3:11.
8. Tim Berners-Lee: *The year open data went worldwide*, Ted 2010, http://www.ted.com/talks/tim_berners_lee_the_year_open_data_went_worldwide.html
9. http://www.ted.com/talks/view/lang/eng//id/788

The Church You Already Belong to

1. *Church Actually*, the Spring Harvest Theme Guide 2012.
2. Romans 15:5–6 NLT.
3. Timothy C. Tennent, *Theology in the Context of World Christianity*, Zondervan, 2007.
4. Yves L. Doz, José Santos and Peter Williamson, *Global to Metanational: How Companies Win in the Knowledge Economy*, Harvard Business Press, 2001, see http://hbswk.hbs.edu/archive/2679.html
5. Makoto Fujimura, *Refractions: A journey of faith, art and culture*, Navpress, 2009 www.makotofujimura.com.

The Future that Already Holds You

1. *Church Actually*, the Spring Harvest Theme Guide 2012.
2. Revelation 7:9–10 NLT.
3. Jurgen Moltmann, *Theology of Hope*, Fortress Press, 1993.
4. Revelation 21:24.
5. Revelation 21:26.
6. *Church Actually*, the Spring Harvest Theme Guide 2012.

Gauguin's Angel

1. *Church Actually*, the Spring Harvest Theme Guide 2012.
2. Mark 16:20 NLT.
3. You can see the picture, and learn about it, at http://en.wikipedia.org/wiki/Vision_After_the_Sermon
4. Andrew Walls, *The Missionary Movement in Christian History*, Orbis, 1996.
5. Andrew Walls in Philip C. Stine, ed., *Bible Translation and the Spread of the Church*, E. J. Brill, 1992.
6. Walls, *The Missionary Movement in Christian History*.

After Athens

1. *Church Actually*, the Spring Harvest Theme Guide 2012.
2. Acts 17:25–26 NLT.
3. Acts 17:24–28.

I See a New City

1. *Church Actually*, the Spring Harvest Theme Guide 2012.

2. Matthew 6:10 NLT.

3. Revelation 21:21; see verse 2.

4. Revelation 21:2 NLT.

5. Revelation 21:3 NLT.

6. Genesis 3:8–9.

7. Leonard Sweet, *twitter comment*, https://twitter.com/#!/lensweet

8. Hebrews 11:9–10 NLT.

9. Ephesians 3:20.

10. *Church Actually*, the Spring Harvest Theme Guide 2012.

11. Revelation 21:5 NLT.

12. © Gerard Kelly 2011.

13. Vinay Samuel, cited in Chris Sugden, *Gospel, Culture and Transformation*, Regnum Books, 1997 and 2000.